Landmark Visitors Guide

Suffolk

Jackie & Mark Mower

D1643307

Published by

Landmark Publishing
Ashbourne Hall, Cokayne Ave, Ashbourne,
Derbyshire, DE6 1EJ, England

Published in the UK by
Landmark Publishing Ltd
Ashbourne Hall, Cokayne Ave, Ashbourne, Derbyshire DE6 1EJ England
Tel: 01335 347349 Fax: 01335 347303
e-mail: landmark@clara.net website: landmarkpublishing.co.uk

1st Edition
ISBN 13: 978-1-84306-389-6

Printed by: Gutenberg Press, Malta

Designed by: Michelle Prost

Edited by: Ian Howe

Front Cover: Thorpeness
Back cover, top: Cavendish
Back cover, middle: Aldeburgh
Back cover, bottom: Monks Eleigh

The images listed below are supplied by Shutterstock with copyright to:
Christopher Hall: Page 11; **Len Green:** Page 6

All other Images supplied by the authors

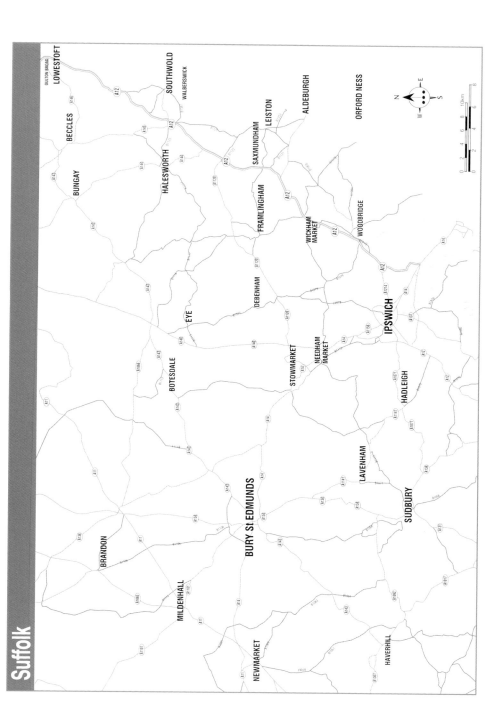

Suffolk

Contents

Opposite page: Martello seascape at sunrise

The county of Suffolk stretches from the chalky downlands of Newmarket in the west to Britain's easternmost point on the coast. North to south, the landscape takes in the lowland forests and sandy brecklands of Brandon to the gently undulating valleys and picturesque beauty that is 'Constable Country'. From its agricultural and maritime roots, Suffolk has remained a county of endearing contrasts: splendidly secluded, yet reassuringly inviting; large and diverse, yet intimately familiar; immediately appealing, yet bewitching for its hidden treasures.

Contrary to popular belief, much of Suffolk's countryside is not flat and uninspiring. There are gently flowing rivers at the bottom of grassy and wooded valleys, rolling hills and narrow twisting lanes leading to small quiet villages. Along the coast there are steeply rising cliffs that fight ongoing battles with the relentless and encroaching waves of the North Sea. This is not a backdrop of quietly forgettable pastures, but a varied landscape that grabs the attention and inspires the creative.

The county has always attracted and

Oulton Broad

7

Top Tips

Ten favourite attractions that should give most visitors a broad appreciation of what Suffolk has to offer:

Brandon, High Lodge Forest Centre
Walks, cycle trails, high ropes course and adventure playground.

Flatford, Bridge Cottage
Thatched cottage at the heart of 'Constable Country'.

Framlingham Castle
Magnificent twelfth-century baronial fortress.

Kessingland, Africa Alive
Top wildlife park.

Lavenham Guildhall
Timber-framed building with museum, tearoom and gift shop.

Long Melford, Kentwell Hall
One of England's finest sixteenth-century houses.

Lowestoft Pleasurewood Hills
Theme park with attractions for all the family.

Minsmere Nature Reserve
Internationally renowned birdwatching area.

West Stow Anglo-Saxon Village
Unique reconstruction of an ancient village on an original archaeological site.

Wetheringsett, Mid-Suffolk Light Railway Museum
Recreated railway with great exhibitions.

beguiled its visitors. Since the end of the last Ice Age it has seen a succession of migrants arrive and settle on its fertile lands and abundant waterways. Yet more have been entranced by the infinite wealth of its long and majestic coastline. Casual sightseers and travelling tourists are a more recent phenomenon, growing in number since the coming of the railways and the dawn of the motor vehicle. Their arrival has opened up the isolated villages and out-of-the-way coastal havens to create a whole new industry for agricultural communities, wooltrade market towns and sea-fishing hamlets that have seen the best and worst of times in their long economic and social history.

Suffolk's splendid seclusion and wide open spaces also mean that wildlife is abundant in this part of the country. From rare and characteristic insects and plant life to unique species of domestic and migratory birds, its natural habitats are both rich and distinctive. Little wonder then that it is home to so many nationally and internationally important Nature Reserves and Areas of Outstanding Natural Beauty.

John Constable, a born and bred Suffolk man, was effusive in his praise for the county's many attractions – what he once referred to as '. . . its gentle declivities, its luxuriant meadow flats sprinkled with flocks and herds, its cultivated uplands, its woods and rivers, with numerous scattered villages and churches, farms and picturesque cottages . . .' Taken together, the environment he painted so affectionately is a place where people can relax and enjoy at leisure the many facets of its historic and natural beauty.

History

Suffolk had its first influx of settlers at least six or seven thousand years ago – the groups of early Stone Age hunter-gatherers who left behind the concentrations of flint tools and waste flakes that still scatter the landscape of The Brecks in the north-western flank of the county. From these early beginnings Suffolk became a favoured home for the late Neolithic people who settled in the fruitful lands of the area. Centuries later, it was the Bronze

and Iron Age inhabitants who began to shape the environment, leaving behind tantalising glimpses of their world at sites around Mildenhall, Bury St Edmunds and West Stow. Beyond this, the Suffolk landscape began to see the development of ordered field systems, roads and defined settlements and the population of the area began to grow.

In the period prior to the Roman invasion, Suffolk began to see iron tools and weapons for the first time. Longer, stronger and sharper, these became the weapons of the military aristocracy, who began to define and defend their specific local areas. The Trinovantes tribe were conquered by the Catuvellauni in south Suffolk at this time. In the north of the county, the Iceni held sway, later to become the stronghold of the warrior queen Boudicca.

The Roman occupation brought new features to both the life and landscape, including military forts, roads, villas, money, written laws, mass-produced pottery, luxury goods from across the Empire and new religious practices like Christianity.

With the collapse of Roman rule in the early fifth century, Anglian settlers from around Holland and the Jutland peninsula migrated into Suffolk, bringing with them new cultural influences. The recreated Anglo-Saxon village at West Stow shows what impact this had on the everyday lives of local people.

The arrival of wandering bands of Danish invaders did much to challenge the growing establishment of Christian settlements throughout Suffolk and Norfolk during the Dark Ages. Like earlier migrants, the Vikings left their mark on the culture and diversity of

Little Hall, Lavenham

Blythburgh Church

Remains of Greyfriars Priory, Dunwich

Beach Huts at Southwold

Southwold beach

the county and their defeat at Hoxne in AD869 of Edmund, King of East Anglia, led to the veneration of one of England's earliest Christian martyrs.

The conversion of local people to Christianity gathered pace from the time of the Norman Conquest, and within twenty years the Domesday Book showed just how many modern-day Suffolk towns and villages were already thriving Christian communities. In defence of their newly acquired lands the feudal barons built defensive keeps and warred with their peers – the physical remains of many of these structures still being evident at places like Bungay, Framlingham and Orford.

Religion continued to dominate the social, economic and political governance of much of East Anglia throughout the Medieval Period. The physical manifestations of this are still apparent – Suffolk retains over 500 parish churches and has more religious buildings per square mile than any other county in Britain.

Equally important at this time was the growing importance of commerce and the wool industry in Suffolk – the extraordinary wealth created by wool merchants leading to the construction and adornment of many hundreds of fine timber-framed houses throughout its market towns. Many of these have survived, largely intact, in places like Lavenham, Kersey, Debenham and Ipswich.

Technological innovations from the late eighteenth century breathed new life into some of the commercial centres of Suffolk which had been hard hit by the decline in agricultural industries. The creation of canals at places like Stowmarket opened up fresh markets to producers and brought in new goods for the growing pre-industrial population.

The arrival and expansion of the rail network in the nineteenth century accelerated this trend, leading to a massive expansion in the fishing ports of Lowestoft, Aldeburgh, Felixstowe and Southwold and opening up these fashionable watering holes to the increasingly affluent Victorian elite.

These changes throughout history have all left their tell-tale signs on the urban and rural landscape. From Neolithic earth mounds to surviving Norman keeps and disused Victorian railway stations, Suffolk has many preserved and hidden treasures waiting to be discovered.

Natural Landscape

The county has a wide range of habitats, rich in all kinds of wildlife. As such, there is always plenty to see. Some of these natural environments – like the Minsmere Nature Reserve and Redgrave and Lopham Fen – are internationally recognised for their distinctive wildlife. Others – like The Brecks and Sandlings – are remarkable for the uniqueness of their habitats, which support large numbers of rare and endangered species. From woodlands to heathlands, coastal estuaries to inland waterways and marshland to chalky downs, Suffolk has some of the best natural environments in Europe.

People

The people of Suffolk have always been resourceful folk who retain a strong sense of their history, identity and traditions. The county can also boast some notable pioneers and artists.

Explorers Bartholomew Gosnold and Thomas Cavendish both had Suffolk roots, as did musician and composer Benjamin Britten. Famous painters John Constable and Thomas Gainsborough were both born in south Suffolk, as were sculptors Thomas Woolner and Maggi Hambling. Suffolk-born writers include George Crabbe, V S Pritchett, Elizabeth Inchbald and Frederick Maurice.

Exploring the Area

Suffolk is one of the safest places to live in the UK and rightly deserves its reputation as a peaceful, largely agrarian, county. With over 3,300 miles (5,400km) of rights of way, its characteristic leafy lanes are a delight to explore by foot, cycle or on horseback and its sleepy secluded villages retain many hidden treasures that are best savoured at a gentle pace.

The county has over 300 places to visit – from castles and windmills to rare breed farms and wildlife parks – some-

thing to suit the interests of almost all visitors, in fact.

Organisation of the Guide

This guide is divided into five area chapters based on the geography of the county – Lowestoft & North-East Suffolk, Ipswich & the Suffolk Coast, Central Suffolk, South Suffolk, and Bury St Edmunds & West Suffolk. Each contains landscapes, towns, villages and features of visitor interest.

In design, the guide has sought to identify those places which visitors will enjoy for their inherent beauty or interest, whether naturally occurring or man-made. Each chapter can be read as a stand-alone section – for those travelling to a specific part of the county – although each contributes to a comprehensive picture of what Suffolk has to offer. Supplementary information and specific points of interest are shown as 'Feature Boxes' and 'Suggested Places to Visit'. The guide also contains a wealth of travel and tourist information in the 'Factfile' section towards the end.

Lowestoft & North-East Suffolk

The north-east corner of Suffolk, which embraces most of what is known locally as the Waveney Valley, is home to some of the best coastal resorts and inland waterways in the county. Alongside some award-winning beaches at Lowestoft, Pakefield, Southwold and Kessingland, the area sits on the edge of The Broads and contains a number of bustling and historic market towns. With abundant facilities for sailing, boating, fishing and canoeing, the area is liked by tourists who favour active excursions, although the attractive and secluded villages, with their winding country lanes, ancient churches and picturesque buildings, also make the location popular with walkers, cyclists and artists.

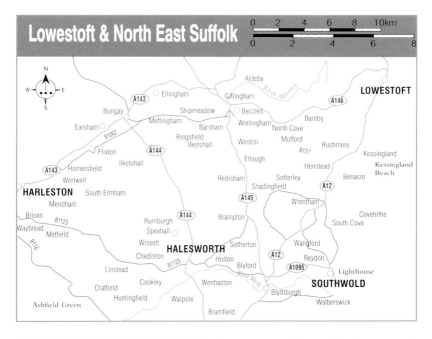

Lowestoft & North East Suffolk

Lowestoft

Lowestoft is the second largest town in Suffolk and occupies the most easterly point in Britain. Alongside its heritage as a popular seaside resort, the town boasts an impressive maritime history and was once one of the largest fishing ports in the world. Today, it continues to be a major centre for commerce and industry, although tourism is playing an increasingly significant part in the economic and social regeneration of the town.

Lowestoft's long, sandy beaches are one of the biggest draws to the area and are watched over by fully trained lifeguards. Often commended for their cleanliness and quality of services, the golden sands attract tens of thousands of tourists each summer. The main beach, which lies close to the town centre, is well served by its seafront **Esplanade**, built largely by the eminent Victorian railway entrepreneur, **Sir Samuel Morton Peto**. It is lined with an impressive stretch of large four- and five-storey Victorian seafront houses, which provide much of the hotel and guest house accommodation in the town. Close by are some attractive public gardens, the **Claremont Pier** and a full range of visitor attractions, which make this one of the most popular family holiday destinations in Suffolk. These attractions include seafront cafes, trampolines and the well-loved Punch and Judy show.

Also along the Esplanade is the impressive **East Point Pavilion**, which

Sir Samuel Morton Peto (1809–98)

Samuel Morton Peto was a pioneering Victorian builder and entrepreneur. At the age of fourteen he inherited his uncle's building firm, learning the trade, and later taking on contracts for work that included Nelson's Column and the Houses of Parliament. From the early 1840s he developed a passion for railways and became a railway contractor, taking on large projects at home and abroad.

In 1843, Peto came to Lowestoft and within four years had established a proper harbour in the town and a railway line that enabled the well-established fishing industry to reach new markets and expand exponentially. A significant part of the town's development south of the harbour came as a result of Peto's vision and investment.

In 1844, Peto bought Somerleyton Hall, near Lowestoft, which he lavishly extended and rebuilt as a huge mansion for himself. In the same decade he became a Liberal Member of Parliament for Norwich and enjoyed his status as one of the most prominent figures in public life. Charles Dickens once came to stay with Peto at Somerleyton Hall and the novel *David Copperfield* is set partly at nearby Blundeston. Descriptions of people living in upturned boats in the novel were based on what Dickens saw during a visit to the Lowestoft Beach Village.

is built largely of glass and styled on an Edwardian pavilion. This houses a large cafe and **Tourist Information Centre**, alongside the imaginative **Mayhem Adventure Play** area – an indoor soft play facility for children which is an ideal place for the younger members of the family to let off steam. The open area outside the building is laid out with some synchronised water fountains which are again popular with visitors. Further south, towards **Pakefield**, Lowestoft has a further stretch of sandy beach with easily accessible snack and ice cream kiosks and inexpensive restaurants.

North of the town, at **Corton**, a wide expanse of beach is set aside for naturists and those wishing to enjoy a little more seclusion. Close by is the significant tourist magnet of **Pleasurewood Hills** theme park, a 50-acre (20-hectare) site with a wide variety of family thrills and rides, and shows involving sea lions, parrots, acrobats and clowns. It continues to be one of the most visited attractions in the whole of East Anglia.

The main shopping area of Lowestoft is largely pedestrianised and provides a wide range of facilities to serve the needs of visitors. The showpiece is the **Britten Centre** – a covered shopping arcade with a variety of modern stores – ideal for picking up holiday supplies and gifts to take home. Elsewhere in the town there is a wide range of sports and leisure facilities.

For those interested in the commercial, maritime and wartime history of the town, Lowestoft again has much to offer. The port is still in operation and lies someway upriver from the main seafront, although a marina area close to the Esplanade provides both permanent and temporary moorings for private pleasure craft. An impressive programme of regeneration is currently underway to expand both the business and tourist potential of the harbour area and revitalise some of the declining commercial interests in the town.

The **Lowestoft and East Suffolk**

Maritime Heritage Museum, the **Lowestoft War Memorial Museum** and the **Royal Naval Patrol Service Association's Naval Museum**, all situated in the **Sparrow's Nest** park along Whapload Road, tell much of the town's recent history; from the rise and fall of the Lowestoft fishing fleet to the local impact of the two world wars. Also noteworthy in this area is **Lowestoft Lighthouse** and the numerous narrow lanes, or **Scores**, which run from the town down to what was the old fishermen's Beach Village in days gone by.

Seasonal events within the town include the two-day annual **Lowestoft Seafront Air Festival** in July and the **Sunrise Coast Lowestoft Grand Carnival Procession and Celebrations** in August.

Someway inland, but adjoined to Lowestoft, is **Oulton Broad**, with its expansive waterway and wide variety of leisure facilities. As an historic site for local boatbuilding, river transportation and commerce, the area has retained many of its original buildings and is particularly popular with those keen on sailing, windsurfing, cruising and sightseeing. Positioned on the edge of The Broads, with its own **yacht station**, mooring facilities and a 'village' of holiday chalets, Oulton Broad is a significant gateway to the inland waterways of both Norfolk and Suffolk.

Oulton Broad is also home to **Nicholas Everitt Park**, which contains a children's play area, crazy golf course, petting zoo and tennis and bowls facilities alongside its watersports amenities. The park also houses a cafe and the **Lowestoft Museum**, which has displays of wartime memorabilia and a collection of traditional Lowestoft porcelain. One of the seasonal attractions at Oulton

Broad is the powerboat racing on the broad itself, with fixtures on Thursday nights during the summer months.

Lowestoft and Oulton Broad are well served by the modern rail network, with three stations and mainline routes to Norwich, Great Yarmouth and London (via Ipswich).

North-west of Lowestoft

Some 5 miles (8km) north-west of Lowestoft is the picturesque village of **Somerleyton**. This hamlet developed largely as a result of Sir Samuel Morton Peto's ownership of nearby **Somerleyton Hall** from 1844 to 1863. He built most of the surrounding homes for workers on the estate and their character and charm has been preserved since that time. Today, Somerleyton Hall is the family home of Hugh Crossley, the great-great-grandson of Sir Francis Crossley, who bought the estate from Peto in 1864. Originally a Jacobean manor, Somerleyton was remodelled into a fine example of an early Victorian Hall in Anglo-Italian style with magnificent carved stonework, sumptuous state rooms and unique wood panelling. The Hall and Gardens (including an impressive maze, beloved of countless generations of children) are open to the public at selected times from April to October.

One of Somerleyton Hall's lesser-known secrets is that it played a part in the development of **Sir Christopher Cockerell's Hovercraft**. Cockerell developed his pioneering plans at a boatyard in Somerleyton. During the 1950s he demonstrated a working model of the hovercraft to Lord Somerleyton on the lawn at Somerleyton Hall. Lord

The Scores of Lowestoft

The Scores are a unique part of Lowestoft's maritime history. They are a series of narrow lanes created over the years by people wearing paths in the soft, sloping cliff as they travelled between the historic High Street and the old fishermen's Beach Village. The word 'score' is believed to derive from the Old English *scora*, meaning to make or cut a line.

Although the Beach Village is gone, the Scores are still of great interest and a 'Scores Trail' (of red herring waymarkers) has been designed to help visitors to understand more of the town's history and the significance of these ancient pathways leading down to the sea.

Somerleyton was impressed and arranged for Cockerell to further demonstrate the model to Lord Mountbatten, then First Lord of the Admiralty. With subsequent backing, Cockerell moved production to the south coast and his prototype SR-N1 was built and crossed the English Channel on 25 July 1959 to widespread acclaim. A roundel on the lawn at Somerleyton Hall marks the spot where Cockerell's model was first demonstrated.

Many of the villages close to Somerleyton – including Herringfleet, Lound and Blundeston – are worth a visit for those into walking, cycling, church history and local hostelries. Given their close proximity to the Norfolk border, they also provide the traveller with easy access to attractions like **Fritton Lake** and the coastline at **Gorleston** and **Great Yarmouth**. Herringfleet is also the site of the last operational **Smock Drainage Mill** in Suffolk. This stands on the River Waveney only a short distance from the local church.

Lowestoft to Beccles

The A146 from Lowestoft to Beccles is a busy tourist route, providing an easy exit for travellers holidaying along the coast who wish to visit the attractive inland market towns of north-east Suffolk and beyond.

The route out of Lowestoft takes visitors through Carlton Colville, on the south-western edge of the town. The **Carlton Marshes Local Nature Reserve** is close by with over 100 acres (40 hectares) of grazing marsh, fens and peat pools. Signposted is the **East Anglian Transport Museum**, which houses an impressive collection of trams, buses and other vehicles from the past, in addition to a bookshop and tearoom. Less than a mile away is the **Rockery Park Golf Course**, which provides unrestricted facilities for visiting golfers during weekdays and at specific times on Saturdays and bank holidays.

Further along the A146 are signs to the village of **Barnby**. The village has a good local pub, **The Swan**, which serves

East Point Pavilion, Lowestoft

a variety of fresh fish dishes from the nearby coast and is popular with tourists and locals alike. Very close to this is the **North Cove Local Nature Reserve** – a wetland habitat housing warblers, siskins and redpolls.

Leaving the A146, en route to Beccles, travellers pass through the village of **Worlingham**, which has become subsumed into the larger town. The local church of **All Saints** is believed to be around 900 years old, although much of what can be seen today is the result of its Victorian restoration. Either way, the attractive building, lychgate and churchyard are worth a visit for those interested in church architecture.

The pretty market town of **Beccles** stands on a hill above the marshes of the River Waveney, close to the border with Norfolk. The town derived its name from the two parts of its present name: 'beck', meaning by the stream, and 'leas', a meadow by the stream.

As a market town, Beccles has a long history. The main church of **St Michael's** dates back to 1369, when the large Gothic building was constructed. On certain days of the year, visitors are able to view the town from the freestanding church tower.

A free school was established in the town in 1631 by Sir John Leman – this is now the site of the **Beccles Museum**, which contains some excellent exhibits documenting the heritage of the town. The **Town Hall** dates back to 1726, and in earlier times held Quarter and Petty Sessions, before becoming a council chamber.

Much of the town's development came as a result of industrialisation in the nineteenth century and, in particular, the coming of the railways from 1860. And while much of the architecture from this period still exists, few of the buildings are now used for their original purpose.

Given its position on the edge of the Norfolk Broads, Beccles is a popular location for anglers, cyclists, walkers and horse riders and those seeking boating and sailing holidays. **Beccles Quay** has mooring facilities and a yacht station and is only a short walk away from the town centre, which is well served by a wide variety of shops, public houses and restaurants and has good rail links to both Lowestoft and Ipswich. There is also a sports centre, swimming pool, indoor bowls centre and snooker hall for public use.

Bungay to Halesworth

The road towards Bungay from Beccles passes through the village of **Mettingham**. A turn-off just beyond the Tally Ho! public house takes the visitor to the earthworks and structural remains of a moated, fortified manor house. **Mettingham Castle** was originally a college for secular priests with a gatehouse, curtain wall and aisled hall. Sadly, little remains of its former glory.

Like Beccles, the attractive market town of **Bungay** stands on Suffolk's border with Norfolk, with extensive views over lush water meadows. The town centre, which is recognised as a Conservation Area by English Heritage, contains a wealth of historic attractions, including a **Roman well, Saxon church, Norman castle** (built by **Hugh Bigod**) and fine lead-domed **Butter Cross**. The distinctive tower of **St Mary's Church** also stands on one of the main thoroughfares of the town. Among its many attractions are the remains of a former priory and the **Druid's Stone**, a granite boulder which may have been used for earlier pagan rituals. It is one of a number of mysterious stones which occupy the Suffolk landscape (see feature box on page 50).

Bungay has a fine range of shops, tearooms, restaurants and public houses. A town **Museum** situated on Broad Street contains a wealth of local memorabilia, including coins, photographs and paintings. The town also has a sports centre, indoor swimming pool and local facilities for the hire of cycles and canoes.

The A144 is the main route from Bungay to Halesworth. Shortly after leaving Bungay, a signpost provides directions to **St Peter's Hall** in South Elmham. The Hall dates from around 1280, but was extended in 1539 using building materials 'robbed' from Flixton Priory, which was dissolved by Cardinal Wolsey in the 1520s. The site is now home to a fine brewery and restaurant.

Within a few miles of this, on the B1062, is the **Norfolk and Suffolk Aviation Museum** at Flixton. This houses over twenty-five historic aircraft, both civil and military, from World War I to the present day, and is popular with families.

Halesworth itself is a bustling market town which lies within an area of rural beauty and isolation, nestled in a curve of the River Blyth. It is well served by the East Suffolk rail line with regular services to Lowestoft and Ipswich. In former years, the town was a major centre for malting, brewing and agriculture and retains many fine buildings, including a carved **Gothic House, Tudor Rectory** and **Elizabethan almhouses**.

The main **Thoroughfare** of the town is now pedestrianised, making shopping and sightseeing relaxed and pleasurable.

At one end of the route is the **Market Place**, where most of the older buildings stand. At the other end is a new public library and, within a few minutes' walk of this, **The Cut** arts centre, with a theatre, cinema and art exhibitions.

Halesworth has a good array of public houses and restaurants and a wide variety of leisure facilities, including a public park, children's play area, skateboard park, heated outdoor pool, bowling green, gym and a nearby eighteen-hole golf course. Close by there is also the **Wisset Wines Vineyard**, which provides tours and tastings. A town **Museum** situated on Station Road contains a variety of artefacts and local information for history buffs. There is also the **Halesworth Airfield Memorial Museum** on Sparrowhawk Road, which houses an extensive collection of World War II memorabilia. This is open on Sundays and bank holidays.

Seasonal events within the town include a local carnival (mid-June), antiques street market (August bank holiday) and a **Gig in the Park** music festival (early August).

Lowestoft to Walberswick

The A12 provides the main route from Lowestoft along Suffolk's heritage coast. Some 4 miles (6km) along this route is the village of **Kessingland**. This former fishing village was an important town as far back as the time of the Domesday Book in 1086, when some 22,000 herrings were being exacted in taxation by the Normans from its local fisheries.

Kessingland's population began to decline with the loss of its harbour, and the Black Death, which ravaged Europe between the fourteenth and

The History of Bungay Castle

The Bigods were an illustrious Norman family who helped with the conquest of England. Roger Bigod assumed control of lands at Bungay, Framlingham and other parts of Suffolk in 1103. Fortifications were built on these sites. In 1120, the property at Bungay was inherited by Roger's son, Hugh.

Hugh Bigod was an ambitious man who became the leader of the warring barons in East Anglia. He had some success in challenging the authority of King Stephen from 1136, securing the title of Earl of Suffolk, but when Henry II acceded to the throne in 1154 a shift in power occurred. The new king took temporary possession of Bigod's lands until 1163, when they were returned to him. However, the Earl's ambition had not deserted him and it was at this time that he began to construct a stone keep at Bungay. With this new stronghold, Bigod joined forces with the Earl of Leicester and, despite some early success, was eventually forced to submit to the King and surrender his lands. Having departed to fight in Syria, Hugh Bigod died around 1178.

The lands at Bungay and Framlingham were eventually restored to the Bigod family by Richard I. Later generations renovated both castles. In 1483, the ownership of Bungay Castle passed to the Howards, Dukes of Norfolk, who retained possession until 1987, when the Castle was presented to the town with an endowment towards its preservation. It is now owned and administered by the Castle Trust. A Castle Visitor Centre was opened in 2000, containing a cafe, displays and gift shop.

seventeenth centuries, killed one in seven of the community's inhabitants. Today, the village relies on the tourist trade, its population almost doubling in the holiday season. It has a long stony beach, holiday camp and caravan site and is popular with holidaymakers and anglers.

On the southern edge of the village is the **Suffolk Wildlife Park – Africa Alive!** which contains a wide variety of wild and farmyard animals, an adventure play area, restaurant and gift shop. It is consistently voted as one of the top family attractions in Suffolk.

A short distance further along the coast is the tiny secluded hamlet of **Covehithe**. Nowhere is the extent of coastal erosion more evident than on its shores, where the cliff top is being washed away at an alarming rate. The area is only accessible along two narrow lanes, one of which runs from the village

of **Wrentham**. Visitors can view the remains of the grand **fifteenth-century church** which stands within the churchyard of the more recent, and much smaller, church of **St Andrew's**. Beyond this, a single-track lane takes visitors to the cliff edge and a coastal path leading to the shoreline. The area is popular with beachcombers and birdwatchers.

Southwold, which sits further south and is accessed from the A12 along three separate routes, is one of the most fashionable of seaside resorts – a status it has retained since the Victorian period. It was incorporated in a charter of Henry VII in 1489 and remains largely unspoilt.

The town has a superb award-winning sandy beach (complete with some of the most sought-after beach huts!) and one of the country's **most famous piers**. The original structure was built in 1900, but suffered damage during a severe storm in 1934 and in World War II. It was restored by its present owner in 2001 and attracts huge visitor numbers.

Not unusually, much of the town's heritage stems from its close association with the sea. The **Battle of Sole Bay** was fought off the coast in 1672, when the English and French fleets clashed with the Dutch navy – a battle involving as many as 50,000 men. Links to this are evident in the town, from the row of cannons on the green at **Gun Hill** to **Sutherland House**, now a hotel and restaurant, which was once the residence of James, Duke of York, brother of Charles II and admiral of the English fleet. Dutch connections include the **Southwold Museum** on Bartholomew Green, a grade II listed building with Dutch gables.

Other landmarks pay homage to the sea. The whitewashed **Southwold Lighthouse**, which began operations in 1890 and still acts as a coastal mark for passing shipping, is open to visitors at key times for much of the year. The **Alfred Corry Museum** on Ferry Road contains exhibits on the ship and maritime history of the area, while the **Sailors' Reading Room**, which was built in 1864, looks out over the golden sands of Southwold beach to the open sea beyond.

Other key attractions include the parish church of **St Edmund's**, which was built in 1460, and the picturesque **harbour area**, once home to a thriving fishing fleet and now beloved of anglers, walkers, sailors and artists. A bridge and separate **foot ferry** enables visitors to cross the River Blyth in order to reach nearby Walberswick.

Southwold is well known for its celebrated **Adnams Brewery**, and has a fine array of public houses, restaurants, galleries, tearooms and shops. Its sea-front attractions include a boating lake, putting green, cafes, ice cream kiosks and amusement arcade.

Further along the A12 route, and some four miles (6km) from Southwold, visitors will encounter the small village of **Blythburgh**. It is set in a landscape of outstanding natural beauty, with a tidal river and a diversity of arable pastures, heath, woodland and marshes. The area itself is well known for its impressive medieval **Church of the Holy Trinity**, which sits just off the main road.

The **White Hart** public house in the village has historical links to the smuggling trade – once endemic in this area of Suffolk – as has the nearby picnic area of **Toby's Walks** on Blythburgh heath.

A seasonal attraction in the area is the **Latitude** music and arts festival weekend at nearby Henham, which takes place in mid-July each year.

Leaving the A12 at Blythburgh, visitors should follow the signs to **Walberswick**, another flourishing port in times gone by and very fashionable as a coastal retreat (almost half of the village's homes are holiday properties). In addition to its long sandy beach, the area has a couple of excellent pubs, an interesting parish church and some good local walks. The village also plays host to the **British National Crabbing Championships** (normally held in August each year), a charity event which attracts large numbers of entrants from all over the world and is a firm favourite with many holidaying families.

Walks in the area

North-east Suffolk is an ideal place for walking. The gently rolling countryside means there are no steep slopes, just inviting rural roads and paths waiting to be explored.

There is an impressive network of promoted walking routes in the area, all waymarked to make them easy to follow. One of the most popular of these is the Angles Way footpath, which runs along the border of Norfolk and Suffolk in the beautiful Waveney Valley, and there are shorter circular routes off this path to discover the quiet countryside and attractive villages of this unspoilt area.

One of the most popular walks in the Lowestoft area is the Easterling Walk from Oulton Broad South to Lowestoft Ness, a two-hour jaunt which takes walkers alongside the open expanses of Oulton Broad and through to the town's most easterly point.

Beccles has a host of rural walks in its surrounding countryside and marshland. Details of these numerous routes can be obtained from the Tourist Information Centre (or viewed on the website www. beccles.biz).

All of the market towns in the area have their own 'town trail' walks. For example, there are two in Bungay (heading westward and eastward) which start at the Market Place and take about two hours to complete.

Halesworth has a pleasant circular walk of 2 miles (3km) across the meadows of its Millennium Green, which sits along the banks of the River Blyth. The route is particularly appealing in spring, when there is an abundance of meadow flowers and local wildlife.

Southwold too has a variety of local walks, including the popular 3-mile (5km) harbour route which starts at Southwold Common and takes walkers along the harbour front (see www. southwold.info for full details of these walks).

Not to be outdone, Walberswick has a wide variety of footpaths and bridleways open to walkers as part of the Suffolk Coast National Nature Reserve. This has over 20 miles (32km) of public rights of way, allowing views of all the diverse habitats along this stretch of coastline. The websites www.eastsuffolklinewalks. co.uk and www.discoversuffolk.org.uk provide further information on the full range of promoted walks in the area.

Cycle Rides

The tranquil rural roads of north-east Suffolk are ideal for cyclists and can take visitors on wonderful journeys of discovery, full of curiosities and sites of interest. Cycle hire is good in the area and Suffolk County Council maintains a highly visible network of cycle routes, including cycle paths in both Lowestoft

Southwold Lighthouse

and Beccles.

Parts of the area fall within some of the National and Regional Cycle Routes. Beccles, Halesworth and South-wold are all on the North Sea Cycle Route (see www.northsea-cycle.com), while Bungay and Halesworth are connected to the Heart of Suffolk Cycle Route.

Car Tours

The five main road routes of the area are those that run from Lowestoft to Beccles (A146), Lowestoft to Blythburgh (A12), Beccles to Bungay (A1062), Beccles to Blythburgh (A145) and Bungay to Halesworth (A144).

Most of the main activities and attractions in and around these routes have already been covered in this chapter. However, the area is not large, so any number of short car tours can be planned around these main routes to discover further hidden gems and secluded areas of the north-east Suffolk countryside.

Public Transport

North-east Suffolk is readily accessible by rail, road and air. The national rail network provides good connections to most of the main towns and there are regular direct services from London via Ipswich on the East Suffolk line.

There are also good internal public transport links and many attractions can be visited by bus (see www.travelineeast-anglia.co.uk or or www.suffolkonboard. com).

In addition, a community transport scheme operates for those unable to travel by conventional public transport as a result of location or mobility impairment. Many of the vehicles used are fully accessible and equipped to carry wheelchairs. The Suffolk County Council Customer Service Centre can provide you with further information on ☎ (0845) 606 6067.

A number of domestic and international flights operate out of Norwich Airport, which is 24 miles (39km) from Beccles and 33 miles (53km) from Lowestoft (on the A146).

Toby's Walks – Picnic Site

Toby's Walks is a perfect spot for picnicking, walking and cycling, with a particularly good view of Blythburgh Church. The name 'Toby's Walks' is attributed to Tobias Gill, a black drummer with the 4th Regiment of Light Dragoons, which was billeted in the Blythburgh area in the summer of 1750 to deal with the excessive smuggling taking place along the coast at that time.

One evening in June 1750, while returning from a drinking bout, Gill met Ann Blakemore, a local barmaid from Walberswick, on the road close to Blythburgh. Folklore has it that he assaulted and murdered the girl before collapsing in a drunken stupor beside her. While the case against Gill was purely circumstantial, he was found guilty of the murder and hanged on Friday 14 September 1750, close to the scene of the crime.

In an ironic twist of fate, it was the local smugglers who did most to preserve the memory of Toby Gill. Inventing numerous ghost tales about 'Black Toby', the smugglers sought to keep people off the local heath as they plied their illicit trade along the highways and waterways of north-east Suffolk.

Places To Visit

(W) = Suggestions for wet days
(C) = Good entertainment value
for children

Africa Alive, Kessingland (C)

Kessingland, Lowestoft, NR33 7TF
☎ (01502) 740291
www.africa-alive.co.uk
Enables visitors to get close to wild animals and discover the sights, sounds and smells of the world's most vibrant and exciting continent. Open: from 10am daily.

Beccles and District Museum (W) (C)

Leman House, Ballygate, Beccles, NR34 9ND
☎ (01502) 715722
www.becclesmuseum.org.uk
Historical displays on the crafts and industries of the area. Open: 2.30pm–5pm Apr–Sep Tue–Sun & BH Mon.

Bigod's Castle, Bungay (C)

Bungay, NR35 2AF
☎ (01986) 896156
www.bungay-suffolk.co.uk/history/castle.htm
Twelfth-century ruins in an elevated position overlooking the River Waveney in the centre of Bungay. Open: Daily.

East Anglian Transport Museum (C)

Chapel Road, Carlton Colville, NR33 8BL
☎ (01502) 518459
www.eatm.org.uk
Working trams, trolley buses in re-constructed 1930s street scene, narrow gauge railway, steam rollers and cars, etc. Open: 11am–5pm Apr–Sep Sun & BHs. 2pm–5pm Jun–Sep Thu & Sat. 2pm–5pm Jul–Sep weekdays except Mon.

Pleasurewood Hills (C)

Leisure Way, Corton, Lowestoft, NR32 5DZ
☎ (01502) 586000
www.pleasurewoodhills.com
Over 40 rides, shows and attractions, set in 50 acres of parkland. Caters for all ages. Open: Apr–Jul specific dates (see website). Jul–Aug daily from 10am. Sep specific dates (see website).

Somerleyton Hall and Gardens (W)

On B1074, five miles NW of Lowestoft
☎ (08712) 224244
www.somerleyton.co.uk
Early Victorian stately mansion in Anglo-Italian style. Lavish architectural features, state rooms, furnishings and paintings. Superb gardens with famous maze. Tearoom and gift shop. Open: Hall 11.30am–4pm Apr–Oct Thu–Sun. Jul–Aug Tue–Wed as well. Gardens 10am–5pm.

Southwold Lighthouse Tours (W)

St James Green, Southwold, IP18 6JL
☎ (01502) 722576
www.trinityhouse.co.uk
Guided lighthouse tour with spectacular views. Open: Selected times Mar–Oct (ring or visit website for details).

Toby's Walks Picnic Site, Blythburgh (C)

On A12/B1387
Lovely picnic site in heathland.
Open: Daily.

Wissett Wines, Valley Farm Vineyards

Wisset, Near Halesworth, IP19 0JJ
☎ (01986) 785535
www.wissettwines.com
Vineyard set in attractive gardens with picnic area, wildlife trail and alpaca herd. Open: 10am–6pm daily.

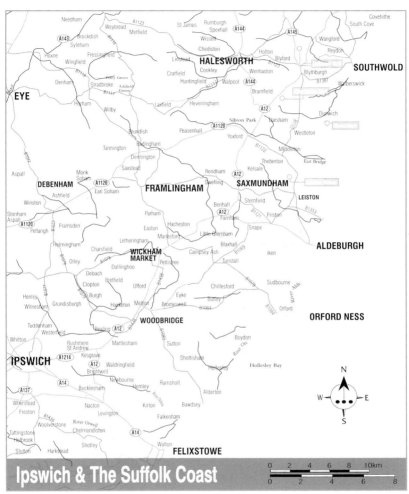

Ipswich & The Suffolk Coast

Aldeburgh Beach

Much of the Suffolk coastline lies within an Area of Outstanding Natural Beauty and is complemented by small market towns and picturesque inland villages. The countryside adjoining this coastline contains no fewer than four major rivers – the Blyth, Alde, Deben and Orwell – and the estuaries of these make water sports a key attraction for visitors. Wildlife and fauna is abundant here and the countryside is both variable and inspiring. Coupled with the history and vibrancy of the county town of Ipswich, the area has much to offer.

Dunwich to Aldeburgh

Many parts of the East Anglian coastline are under the threat of erosion from the sea. And yet, as the experience of **Dunwich** shows all too clearly, this is hardly a new phenomenon. The town lies south of Walberswick in a peaceful and secluded area of countryside.

Dunwich Beach, with its stony banks, inland estuary and scattered fishing boats, evokes memories of a time gone by. The sleepy coastal haven is a must for birdwatchers, walkers and those with a penchant for medieval church history. The tiny, but hugely informative, **Dunwich Museum** on the main street provides visitors with a good understanding of the town's rise and fall.

Elsewhere, tourists can visit the ruins of a **Greyfriars Monastery** and the church of **St James**, which also contains remnants of an earlier leper hospital. In the springtime, the woodland close to these sites is awash with a carpet of snowdrops and bluebells, making for a particularly pleasant ramble.

The expansive **Dunwich Heath** area contains a diversity of natural environments, from heathland and shoreside walks to shady woods and sandy cliffs. It is also home to some rare species, including the elusive Dartford warbler and antlion – the latter only being found in this area of the **Suffolk Sandlings**. Ramblers, dog walkers and picnickers can also spend many hours enjoying the vast and well-maintained area of **Dunwich Forest,** which lies at the entrance to the town.

Closer to the A12, and not far from Darsham, there is another area of forest that is popular with tourists. **High Lodge** in Hinton has 100 acres of woodland complete with holiday lodges, clay pigeon shooting, a golf course and fishing lakes.

A little further south-east of this, nature lovers can explore further tracts of the Sandlings on the **Westleton Heath Nature Reserve**. This area is home to tree pipits, stonechats and nightjars, alongside some rare solitary

Dunwich – The Lost City

Dunwich was a settlement in Roman times and by the seventh century was a town of considerable wealth. In 1086, its population stood at 3,000 and the community had no fewer than six parish churches. By the thirteenth century it could claim to be more important than the town of Ipswich, providing a safe harbour at the mouth of the Blyth estuary and supporting a thriving boat building industry.

The town's vulnerability to coastal erosion eventually led to its downfall and a hurricane in January 1328 drove a spit of shingle inland to block the harbour entrance. From this point on the town's fortunes waned. Throughout the remainder of the century the sea ravaged the fragile coastline, taking as many as 400 homes, two churches and numerous shops, until much of Dunwich lay underwater – truly a tale of a 'lost city'.

bees and wasps.

The village of **Westleton** has some attractions of its own. The **Crown Inn** serves some excellent food and is the oldest working coaching inn in England. A coach and horses can be hired from the inn for countryside trips. The area also has a quaint village green and duck pond. One of its popular seasonal events is an annual **barrel race** on the green.

In close proximity is the internationally renowned **Minsmere Nature Reserve**, which is rich in all kinds of wildlife but is a haven for birdwatchers. The site has a visitor centre with excellent facilities and considerable efforts have been made to open up many parts of the reserve to disabled people.

A short distance inland, the village of **Wenhaston** itself holds a hidden gem. The local church contains a rare medieval panel showing souls being selected to go to Heaven or Hell. The '**Wenhaston Doom**' is believed to have been painted by a monk at nearby Blythburgh Priory around 1480.

Theberton – Crash Site of a Zeppelin

It was at daybreak, on the morning of 17 June 1917, that one of Germany's most prized Zeppelin airships, the L48, crashed to earth in a ball of flame near the village of Theberton. From the crew of nineteen, only three men survived. They became the first, and last, German airmen to survive the crash of a burning airship over enemy territory. The deceased were buried in the local churchyard, where they remained for the next forty-nine years until their bodies were removed and taken to the German national war cemetery in Staffordshire.

At the time, in an age before global and up-to-the-minute news coverage, the event pushed the small community into the limelight and the national press. The shooting down of the Zeppelin was a visible and lasting reminder that no part of Britain, not even the sleepy, out-of-the-way villages of rural Suffolk, would ever again be immune from the ravages of total warfare.

The main route from Westleton towards Leiston (on the B1125/B1122) takes travellers through the village of **Theberton**. This was the scene of one of the most remarkable air incidents of World War I, when a German Zeppelin was shot down over the village. Remnants of the aircraft are still displayed in the local church of **St Peter's**.

Further along the B1122 from Theberton is the site of **Leiston Abbey**. This was founded in 1182 and was originally on a small island surrounded by water. Some visible ruins of a chapel remain. Not far away are signposts to Sizewell. The beach here is secluded and local campsites attract a fair number of visitors. The area sits within the shadow of Sizewell B nuclear power station.

The nearby town of **Leiston** was made famous by the Garrett engineering works, which produced agricultural, industrial and military machinery for

Fishing Boats on Aldeburgh Beach

hundreds of years. The works now form part of the **Long Shop Museum**, which provides plenty of entertainment for children and adults alike.

The town itself is well equipped with a cinema, shops, restaurants, public houses and a large sports centre. Close by, there are also the remains of **Leiston Airfield**, which served as an important allied airbase in World War II. Sadly, only a few of its original buildings

Moot Hall, Aldeburgh

still exist, lying overgrown and largely neglected.

Saxmundham is only a couple of miles away from the airfield. This small market town is on the main A12 route towards Ipswich and has a railway station on the East Suffolk line. Among its attractions is **Saxmundham Museum**, which has a small cinema showing films of past times and a 'touch screen' computer with old photographs of the town.

Those heading further south of Leiston on the B1122 will see signposts to **Thorpeness** on the B1353. The village was originally a small fishing hamlet with a reputation for being a major smuggling route into East Anglia. Its real growth began in 1910 when **Glencairne Stuart Ogilvie**, a wealthy Scottish barrister, bought a sizeable proportion of land in the area. He developed Thorpeness into a private fantasy holiday village, to which he invited his family and friends in the summer months.

Today, the visible reminders of his vision include the five-storey '**House in the Clouds**' and an artificial boating lake, known as **Thorpeness Meare**, based on a Peter Pan theme (the writer **J M Barrie** was a close friend of Ogilvie's). The village is a great place for children and the annual regatta and fireworks display in late August attracts large numbers of visitors.

Also worth a visit is the **Thorpeness Post Mill**, which was moved to its present location (opposite the House in the Clouds) in the winter of 1922 from the nearby village of Aldringham. Restored in the 1970s, the mill is now used as a visitor centre for the Suffolk

House in the Clouds, Thorpeness

Coast and Heaths Area of Outstanding Natural Beauty.

Alongside Southwold, **Aldeburgh** is widely seen as a jewel in the crown of Suffolk's coastal resorts. Its name in old English means 'old fort' and, like Dunwich, most of its original Tudor buildings have been lost to the sea.

Aldeburgh has a long shingle beach on which can be seen a few remaining fishing boats and the more recent memorial to musician/composer **Benjamin Britten** – a twelve-foot (3.5m) high **scallop shell sculpture** in stainless steel by artist **Maggi Hambling**. Both hint at the rich diversity of culture and social history which the town exemplifies.

Benjamin Britten lived here for thirty years and it is easy to see why. The quiet, genteel nature of the town belies its vibrancy as a seaside watering hole. There are good restaurants, public houses and gift shops interspersed with art galleries and a couple of the best fish and chip shops in Suffolk.

Moot Hall, a surviving timber-framed Tudor building, is arguably the town's most recognisable landmark. This doubles up as both a town hall and museum, containing a wealth of local artefacts. Further along the coastline is a Napoleonic **Martello Tower** with a unique quatrefoil design. The endless battering of the waves is now threatening its survival and coastal erosion has already removed the seaward side of its outer defences.

Aldeburgh has long been recognised for its associations with Benjamin Britten and the **Aldeburgh Festival**, which he founded in 1948. This eventually outgrew its birthplace and is now

Snape Maltings and Benjamin Britten

Snape Maltings is best known for its concert hall, which is one of the main sites of the annual Aldeburgh Festival. Most of its buildings date from the nineteenth century, when the site was a centre for malting barley in the brewing of beer. It closed for this purpose in 1960. Since that time the buildings have been partially restored and converted into shops, galleries and the concert hall.

The concert hall is well known for its connections with composer Benjamin Britten. He was born in Lowestoft in 1913, the son of a dentist and a talented amateur musician. His status as one of the country's greatest composers is now secure, although during the 1930s he set himself apart from the English musical mainstream, which he regarded as inward-looking and amateurish.

held annually in June at the **Snape Maltings** concert hall. The Maltings site also has a number of shops and galleries, a restaurant and tearoom. The tranquillity of the area is best enjoyed on the nearby river walk or the boat trip available from the quayside.

Orford to Martlesham

Heading south out of Snape Maltings, travellers are presented with the opportunity to head back towards the sea in the direction of **Orford**. The town grew up around its twelfth-century **Royal Castle** and the ninety-foot (27m) Norman keep survives, largely intact, as one of the finest in Britain. The views from the top provide visitors with a magnificent outlook over the river and surrounding countryside.

Orford has a fine range of interesting buildings and a small local **Museum**. The quay area has good public houses and restaurants and provides boat trips out to **Havergate Island**, an RSPB bird sanctuary, and **Orford Ness**, a shingle spit of land off the main coastline. The site is an internationally important nature reserve with some of the rarest wildlife and plants in the country. Set within its peaceful surroundings are also the buildings, craters and equipment of a secret military testing site which was established in 1913.

The route out of Orford on the B1084 and B1078 passes **Tunstall Forest**. The area consists of coniferous plantations, broadleaved belts and heathland areas, which link up with both **Tunstall** and **Blaxhall Common**. These areas are very good for sightings

Shingle Street – A Wartime Enigma

British wartime conspiracy theories are nothing new. One such story has been the enduring mystery surrounding an alleged Nazi invasion in August 1940 along the windswept coastline of Shingle Street.

That something happened off the coast on the night of Saturday 31 August 1940 is not disputed. Eyewitnesses claimed that around 9pm there was a tremendous amount of gunfire and explosions and the night sky was lit up with a red glow. This sporadic gunfire went on for several hours. Rumours at the time suggested that a German invasion had been attempted and a number of locals claimed later that they had seen burned bodies along the shoreline – bodies dressed in German Wehrmacht uniforms.

The story of a German invasion along the Suffolk coast has certainly been a persistent legend, which has inspired numerous works of fiction and a number of authoritative texts, not least of which was Peter Haining's 2004 book '*Where the Eagle Landed*'. What is certain is that the threat of an enemy attack was taken seriously at the time.

of ground nesting birds like the nightjar and woodlark. The area is very popular with walkers, cyclists and horse riders and twice-yearly hosts a **Motorcycle Enduro** event organised by the Woodbridge & District Motorcycle Club.

Further south of Tunstall is another woodland area providing a range of activities. **Rendlesham Forest**, on the B1084, covers some 1,500 hectares and contains both picnic sites and recreation areas. There is an 'easy access' walking trail and two family cycle trails, which are waymarked, and cover distances of 6 miles (10km) and 10 miles (16km).

Back towards the sea, there is an intriguing and largely overlooked area of the coastline south-east of this, known as **Shingle Street**. This is one of the most isolated villages in Suffolk. It consists of a row of isolated cottages built along a wide stretch of stones and pebbles which have been thrown up by the sea to form a high bank. The desolate hamlet has no shops, pub or church, al-though it retains a few holiday homes. It was the location for one of the strangest mysteries of World War II, when it was claimed that a number of burnt bodies in German uniforms were washed up on the shore and removed in secrecy.

The main town in this area is **Woodbridge**, which is set on the banks of the River Deben and just across the river from one of the most important Anglo-Saxon sites in Britain – the **Sutton Hoo** royal burial ship. Sutton Hoo is a group of low grassy mounds close to the river. A permanent visitor centre is situated on the site, off the B1083 Woodbridge to Bawdsey road.

Woodbridge itself is easily reached by road or rail and retains a wealth of interesting and historic buildings. It has 1,400 years of recorded history and is famous for its **Tide Mill**, which dates from the eighteenth century and contains three floors of exhibits and working models. **Woodbridge Museum** provides a comprehensive set

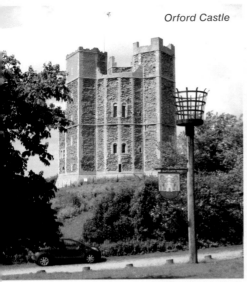

Orford Castle

Tide Mill, Woodbridge

and **Bawdsey Manor**, which became a top-secret research establishment in 1936, was the birthplace of Radar technology. A **ferry service** from Felixstowe operates to take passengers across the River Deben to Bawdsey.

Martlesham sits on the A12 between

Thorpeness Windmill

of exhibits which tell the story of the town, while the six-storey **Buttram's Windmill**, close to Market Hill, is considered to be one of England's finest tower windmills. Elsewhere on Market Hill is the **Shire Hall**, which has been the focal point of the town for over 400 years. It houses the **Heavy Horse Museum**, an award-winning museum dedicated to the Suffolk Punch horse breed.

As a shopping location, Woodbridge is first-rate and has a good blend of shops along its main street, **Thoroughfare**. The town is well catered for in terms of public houses, restaurants and other eateries and there is also a good sports and leisure centre close to the railway station.

Directly south of Woodbridge is the **Bawdsey Peninsula**. This provides fine views of the sea and has two **Martello Towers** situated close by. The area is indeed rich in military history – it was heavily defended in World War II

The Sutton Hoo Treasure

In 1939, local archaeologist Basil Brown excavated an ancient mound and unearthed Anglo-Saxon ship rivets, leading to one of the most amazing discoveries of this country's history. It was the ultimate find, the ship burial of an Anglo-Saxon warrior king and his most treasured possessions, missed by grave robbers and lying undisturbed for over 1,300 years. The treasure belonged to one of the earliest English kings, Redwald, King of East Anglia.

Thorpeness Meare

Quayside at Snape Maltings

Woodbridge and Ipswich. It is actually a settlement of two parts: the older part lying, as it has for centuries, along the River Finn and the A1214, while the newer Martlesham Heath area sits high on a windswept heath which was once the home of a military airfield. The **Martlesham Heath Control Tower Museum** is located off Deben Avenue and tells the fascinating story of the airbase, from its origins in World War I to its eventual closure in 1963.

Elsewhere, at the bottom of the steep Martlesham Hill and close to the river, stands the **Red Lion**, an ancient coaching inn which has served as a landmark to countless generations of Suffolk folk.

For younger visitors, Martlesham has a **Family Entertainment Centre** on Gloster Road, with a tenpin bowling alley for children, a 26,000 square foot jungle-themed indoor adventure play area and a state-of-the-art laser gun maze. Not far away is **Beacon Valley Karts**, on Bealings Road, an exciting off-road track on a six-acre site, which offers three different-sized karts and tracks for different age groups.

Ipswich

As the county town of Suffolk, **Ipswich** has an extensive history and is in fact the longest continuously occupied Anglo-Saxon town in England. Starting life as a small Saxon trading settlement in the early seventh century, 'Gippa's Wic' or 'Gip's Wic' soon developed into a flourishing port with trade links to Germany and many other parts of Europe. The wool trade, in particular, provided a good living for local farmers, textile workers, merchants and sailors.

The great **Cardinal Wolsey**, First Minister to King Henry VIII, was a key resident.

Ipswich has something for everyone. There are twelve medieval churches in the town, including the one used by the **Tourist Information Centre** (St Stephen's). A stroll around the town centre is more than just a pleasant walk; it is an architectural feast that illustrates the town's culture and trade throughout the centuries. The diverse buildings range from the **Ancient House**, with its fine exterior pargeting (see feature box on page 64), to Sir Norman Foster's modern **Willis Building**, reflecting the ease with which the old blends in with the new.

Across Arras Square, visitors can enter

Cardinal Wolsey – An Ipswich Man

Thomas, Cardinal Wolsey was born in Ipswich in the early 1470s. It is often said that his father was a local butcher, although this story is likely to have been invented to undermine the position and status of Thomas, who rose to become a leading statesman and First Minister to King Henry VIII.

When Henry became king in 1509, Wolsey became a controlling figure, attaining the position of Lord Chancellor and Cardinal in 1515. His role gave him significant freedom and power and he built himself a palace at Hampton Court which rivalled that of many monarchs at the time and which would later be occupied by English kings. He died in November 1530.

the **Buttermarket Shopping Centre**. This circular feature contrasts well with the surrounding historic buildings and is popular with gift-seekers. The walk up St Stephen's Lane takes sightseers past the Grade I-listed splendour of the Ancient House and across a road into Dial Lane, site of the fifteenth century **Church of St Lawrence**.

At the end of Dial Lane is the modern entrance to the **Tower Ramparts Shopping Centre**. A left turn here takes visitors along Tavern Street and past **The Walk**, a lively collection of shops in the Tudor style of the early 1930s. At the end of Tavern Street is the open area of the Cornhill, the very centre of the town and the site of civic ceremonies, fairs and street markets. Alongside the grand **Town Hall**, which was built in 1868 of Bath stone, red sandstone and Portland limestone, the area contains the **Golden Lion Hotel** and **Mannings** public house – both timber-framed buildings with later fronts.

Behind the Town Hall is the old **Corn Exchange**, built between 1878 and 1882 and now an arts and entertainment centre (including the **Ipswich Film Theatre**). Ipswich can rightfully claim to be the entertainment capital of the county, with its own acclaimed arts festival, the biggest theatre in the region, the **Cardinal Park** nightlife and cinema zone, classical civic concerts and a free music day in **Christchurch Park**.

Christchurch Mansion, which sits within the grounds of Christchurch Park, north-east of the town centre, is a fine red-brick Tudor building and one of the most important attractions in Suffolk. It is built on the site of a twelfth-century Augustinian priory, which suffered at the hands of Thomas Cromwell, who ransacked it during Henry VIII's dissolution of the monasteries in 1528. Today the property is home to a fine collection of art and period furniture, including paintings by the Suffolk artists Thomas Gainsborough and John Constable and many others.

In addition to its entertainment and arts credentials, Ipswich can also boast some good museums. The **Ipswich Museum** on the High Street has exhibits covering the town's Roman and Anglo-Saxon heritage and an interesting collection of Sikh artefacts. There are also geology and wildlife displays in addition to some topical, one-off, exhibitions. In contrast, the **Ipswich Transport Museum** on Cobham Road sits within an old trolleybus depot and displays a wide range of trams, buses, wagons, bicycles and engineering products. Many of the exhibits were built locally.

Also offering lots of local flavour are the **Tolly Cobbold Brewery Museum** on Cliff Road, which runs guided tours of the company's traditional brewing facilities, and the **Clifford Road Air Raid Shelter Museum**, which houses a fascinating collection of wartime memorabilia.

As a modern, vibrant town, Ipswich has a wide range of sporting facilities, including golf courses, swimming pools and an impressive **Dry Ski Slope** at nearby Wherstead. For spectators, **Ipswich Town Football Club** play at the Portman Road stadium and speedway fans can watch the local **Ipswich Witches** side racing at Foxhall Heath.

On the leisure front, Ipswich has a thriving night-time economy of restaurants, bars and nightclubs. Much of this is located on **The Waterfront**, where hotels, eateries and marinas have replaced the old industrial skyline. One of the best ways to see the regenerated Neptune Dock is by taking one of the regular **public cruises** which operate on the quayside from Easter to the end of September.

For those who prefer the peace and tranquillity of the countryside, the area surrounding Ipswich holds many attractions. There are ten Local Nature Reserves covering various areas of the Gipping Valley, such as **Fen Alder Carr**, **Bramford Meadows** and **Stoke Park Wood**. Some of these contain picnic sites and provide access for pushchairs and wheelchair users.

In terms of seasonal attractions, Trinity Park, on Felixstowe Road just outside Ipswich, hosts the county's biggest annual event. The **Suffolk Show**, which is held at the end of May or in early June, provides grand ring displays and 700 trade stands, flower and art shows, a rural craft marquee and food hall, children's farm and sports area together with a tourism village, livestock and equestrian events.

Felixstowe to East Bergholt

Felixstowe, to the south-east of Ipswich, is a resort that retains much of its original Edwardian charm. The beach is a mixture of sand and shingle and the traditional seafront amenities are popular with its many seasonal visitors. They include the **Spa Pavilion Theatre**, which has an excellent programme of shows throughout the year, with top names during the summer season.

Also on the seafront is an excellent modern **Leisure Centre**, which is open all year round and has flumes and slides for its many family visitors. Together with the **Brackenbury Sports Centre** on High Street East, with its tennis, squash, and badminton facilities, it ensures that the town is

Theberton Church

Westleton Green

well catered for. The latter also has an Ofsted-registered crèche.

In Roman times, the cliffs at Felixstowe stretched out to sea for a further mile and much of the town's history has resulted from its position as a coastal defence point. In 1338, Edward III used the long creek, now known as Kingsfleet, to assemble his fleet before setting off to engage with the French. **Landguard Fort** marks the spot where England was last invaded, in 1667. Alongside the fort, the site is home to a **Nature Reserve** and **Museum.**

It was in the second half of the nineteenth century that Felixstowe began its rapid growth. Much of this was the result of its tourist industry, which made the town a fashionable watering hole. The other reason was the creation of

Willy Lott's Cottage, Flatford

the port in 1886. Felixstowe is now the largest container port in Europe and operates a successful **ferry service** to the continent.

West of Felixstowe across the River Orwell is the **Shotley Peninsula**. The Orwell and Stour rivers form the upper and lower boundaries of this wedge-shaped piece of land, which extends for a distance of some 35 miles (56km). Most of the villages in the area lie close to the river estuaries and there is a public path along much of the coastline, offering excellent views. From Ipswich, the peninsula can be entered by passing under the **Orwell Bridge**.

One of the highlights of the area is **Pin Mill**, which has retained its earlier maritime charm and features a boatyard, cottages, old barges and the seventeenth-century **Butt & Oyster** public house. This has strong smuggling connections and featured in a number of books by **Arthur Ransome**.

Other popular attractions on the peninsula include the **Royal Hospital School**, near Holbrook, the **HMS Ganges Association Museum** on Shotley Marina and the **Alton Water Sports Centre** with sailing and windsurfing facilities.

At its widest part, the peninsula encompasses almost the whole of what is universally known as 'Constable Country'. **John Constable** was born in East Bergholt and visitors can still see the landscapes that inspired him. For those wishing to get a close-up view of the landscape here, it is possible to pack up a picnic and row down the river at **Flatford Mill** – part of a hamlet that includes **Willy Lott's Cottage**. The mill is now a field studies centre and the tourist facilities in the area are run by the National Trust. These include a teashop, guided tours, boat hire, a museum and a large car park.

East Bergholt itself is a village of large elegant houses, which give some indication of the wealth created by their wool merchant owners. Well worth a visit is the **East Bergholt Place Garden**, set in twenty acres (8 hectares) and containing many rare plants and shrubs and an arboretum.

Walks in the Area

The Ipswich and Suffolk coastal area is a fantastic place to explore on foot and there are routes suitable for all levels of interest and ability – from serious long-distance routes to short strolls around the towns or countryside. The area has an excellent network of footpaths and bridleways, large areas of open access land, varied terrain and many points of interest.

Three main long-distance routes are:

1. The Suffolk Coast and Heaths Path

This runs from Felixstowe to Lowestoft covering a distance of 50 miles (80km) in easy stages. It is a stunning walk through the ancient and tranquil land-

John Constable – Landscape Painter

John Constable was born in East Bergholt on 11 June 1776. His father, Golding Constable, was a wealthy miller and businessman who owned watermills at Flatford and Dedham and a windmill at East Bergholt. It was in this area, now known affectionately as 'Constable Country', that the artist produced some of his most celebrated pictures as an English Romantic painter.

In his youth, Constable embarked on amateur sketching trips in the Dedham Vale. He once said that the Suffolk countryside 'made me a painter, and I am grateful'. He started studying at the Royal Academy in 1799 and for the next ten years earned a small amount of money as a probationer, copying pictures and doing portraits. From 1803 he began to be exhibited in his own right. He was eventually elected to the Royal Academy in 1829.

Constable married his childhood sweetheart, Maria Bicknell, in 1816 and settled in Hampstead. The couple had seven children. When Maria died in 1828, it marked the end of Constable's most productive period of painting. He died on 31 March 1835.

Despite the affection for his work, Constable only sold twenty paintings in England throughout his career. In fact, he had far greater success in France. Largely as a result of the pictures he painted of the Suffolk countryside, he has become recognised as one of England's finest landscape artists.

scapes of the Suffolk coastline.

2. The Sandlings Walk

A 60-mile (97km) walk between the eastern fringes of Ipswich and South-wold, linking the remaining fragments of the beautiful Sandlings Heath – Brit-ain's rarest wildlife habitat.

3. The Stour and Orwell Walk

A walk around two of the most beauti-ful estuaries in East Anglia. The route covers 42 miles (68km), starting at Felixstowe and covering the area cel-ebrated by artists, poets and writers.

The area is included on the follow-ing Ordnance Survey maps: Landranger 1:50,000 series (red cover), sheets 156 and 169; and Explorer 1:25,000 series (orange cover), sheets 231, 212 and 197. The maps show all the current rights of way and information about open access land.

There are also a vast number of shorter walks across the area. The selec-tion below gives some indication of the diversity of routes to choose from:

1. RSPB Minsmere Nature Reserve

Two circular trails of just over a mile (2 km) through marsh, woodland and beach habitats.

2. Ipswich Town Centre

Fully guided tours of the town centre leaving the Tourist Information Centre every Tuesday and Thursday at 2.15pm from May to the end of September.

3. Orwell County Park

Waymarked trails around 150 acres (60 hectares) overlooking the River Orwell.

4. Walking around Felixstowe

Seven circular routes of between 3 and 7 miles (5–8km) around the town, with views of the sea and Deben estuary.

5. A walk around Alton Water

A ramble around the Alton reservoir on the Shotley Peninsula.

Route maps for all of these can be obtained from Tourist Information Centres.

Cycle Rides

Cycling is both easy and rewarding in this part of the county. The area is relatively low-lying and contains few challenging hills, making it suitable for even the most occasional of cyclists. Routes are well-marked (many off road) and cycle hire is easy.

Many of the trains on the East Suffolk line have bicycle facilities and the sta-tions have bike racks. At Ipswich station there are cycle lockers and rail operator National Express East Anglia even offers a bicycle rescue service for cyclists in the county. In addition, there are foot and cycle ferries between Felixstowe and Shotley and across the Deben Estuary on the ferry from Felixstowe to Bawdsey. Further north there is a footbridge and foot ferry over the River Blyth between Walberswick and Southwold.

The area has some excellent cycle routes, including the Suffolk Coastal Cycle Route – a 75-mile (120km) circular route from the north of Felix-stowe to Dunwich and Snape – and the Sustrans Route 1, which cuts across to the Suffolk coast on its way down to Felixstowe.

Tourist Information Centre, St Stephen's Church, Ipswich

Ancient House, Ipswich

Flatford Mill

Car Tours

The A12 is the main trunk road from Ipswich (or Lowestoft) to all areas of the Suffolk coastline and the quickest way to get around. Short car tours off this route to the individual towns and villages on the coast rarely take more than fifteen minutes.

There are two particular car tours which visitors should consider:

1. Blythburgh to Aldeburgh

When heading towards Ipswich on the A12, take the turn-off just beyond the Blythburgh White Hart and join the B1125 towards Westleton. The route can be followed through Theberton and Leiston, before joining the B1353 through Thorpeness and into Aldeburgh. It takes in a wide variety of country and seaside views and should take no more than forty minutes.

2. A trip around Shotley Peninsula

When heading towards Ipswich, leave the A12 just before the Orwell Bridge and follow the signs to Shotley. The B1456 is the main route towards Pin Mill and Shotley Gate, where there are superb seaside views. Heading back on the road overlooking Holbrook Bay will enable visitors to take in Alton Water. Allow three hours with stopping time.

Public Transport

There are good air, sea, road and rail links to Ipswich and the wider Suffolk coast. Ipswich is only 47 miles (76km) from Norwich airport and 50 miles (80km) from London Stansted. By sea,

Remains of Leiston Abbey

there are daily sea crossings to Belgium and Holland from Harwich – only 32 miles (51km) from Ipswich – and passenger ferries are also available to Denmark and other countries.

On the roads, National Express operates a daily service to Ipswich from London Victoria, Manchester, Sheffield and Nottingham. The coach station in Ipswich is conveniently situated in the town centre.

In addition, a community transport scheme operates for those unable to travel by conventional public transport as a result of location or mobility impairment. The Suffolk County Council Customer Service Centre can provide you with further information on ☎ (0845) 606 6067.

For car drivers, a convenient park and ride service operates from three sites across Ipswich, with connections to the town centre every ten minutes. These are all signed from major routes. There are over 500 spaces at each site, including dedicated areas for families and disabled drivers. The service includes low-floor buses for easy boarding, money-saving Smartcard tickets and special group travel offers. Shopping trolleys and wheelchairs are available for loan if required.

Trains from London Liverpool Street reach Ipswich in just over an hour. The main East Coast line (serving the north of England and Scotland) connects with an Ipswich service at Peterborough. The East Suffolk line from Ipswich provides good connections to most of the larger inland towns along the Suffolk coastal area and a separate branch line operates services to Felixstowe. Ipswich railway station is a short walk away from the town centre and just two minutes away by bus.

Beach Huts at Felixstowe

Places To Visit

(W) = Suggestions for wet days
(C) = Good entertainment value for children

Aldeburgh Museum (W) (C)

The Moot Hall, Sea Front, Aldeburgh
☎ (01728) 454666
www.aldeburghmuseum.org.uk
Town and maritime history in a sixteenth-century timber-framed hall.
Open: 2.30pm–5pm Apr Sat & Sun. 2.30pm–5pm May & Sep daily. 12pm–5pm Jun–Aug daily.

Bridge Cottage and Dedham Vale, Flatford

East Bergholt, Suffolk, CO7 6UL
☎ (01206) 298260
www.nationaltrust.org.uk
Sixteenth-century thatched cottage at the very heart of Constable Country. Enjoy the pretty backdrop of Flatford Mill and Willy Lott's Cottage and stand on the very spot where Constable painted *The Hay Wain*.
Open: 11am–5pm Mar & Apr Wed–Sun. 10.30am–5.30pm May–Sep daily. 11am–4pm Oct daily. 11am–3.30pm Nov & Dec Wed–Sun. 11am–3.30pm Jan & Feb Sat & Sun.

Christchurch Mansion (W) (C)

Christchurch Park, Ipswich, IP4 2BE
☎ (01473) 433554
Historic sixteenth-century house set in Christchurch Park. Rooms furnished in Tudor through to Victorian periods. Best collection of Constable and Gainsborough paintings outside London.
Open: 10am–5pm Apr–Sep Tue–Sat. 2.30pm–4.30pm Sun.

Landguard Fort

Viewpoint Road, Felixstowe, IP11 8TW
☎ (07749) 695523
Eighteenth-century fort with later additions overlooking Harwich harbour.
Open: Times vary (ring for specific details).

Leiston Abbey

Off the B1122
Fascinating remains of a fourteenth-century abbey.
Open: Daily.

Long Shop Museum, Leiston (W) (C)

Main Street, Leiston, IP16 4ES
☎ (01728) 832189
www.longshop.care4free.net
A wealth of exhibits and history from Leiston's unique past.
Open: 10am–5pm Apr–Oct Mon–Sat. 11am–5pm Sun.

Martlesham Family Entertainment Centre (W) (C)

Gloster Road, Martlesham Heath (just off the A12)

☎ (01473) 611111 (Kingpin) and (01473) 611333 (Laserking and Kidz Kingdom)

Provides tenpin bowling for children, a 26,000 square foot jungle-themed indoor adventure play area and a laser gun maze. Food, ice creams, soft drinks and birthday party packages are also available.

Open: Daily.

Minsmere Nature Reserve (C)

Westleton IP17 3BY

☎ (01728) 648281

www.rspb.org.uk

Internationally renowned birdwatching area in a beautiful stretch of coastline with woods, beach, cliff and heathland.

Open: Daily.

Orford Castle (W) (C)

In the centre of Orford

☎ (01379) 450472

www.english-heritage.org.uk

Visit the great keep of this Royal Castle and enjoy the spectacular views of Orford Ness.

Open: 10am–6pm Apr–Sep. 10am–4pm Oct–Mar Thu–Mon.

Snape Maltings (W)

Off the A12, four miles (6km) from Aldeburgh

☎ (01728) 688303

www.snapemaltings.co.uk

Unique collection of Victorian buildings beside the River Alde, housing beautiful gifts and furniture. Includes a gallery, shops and a public house.

Open: 10am–5pm daily

Sutton Hoo (C)

Off the B1083 Woodbridge to Bawdsey road

☎ (01394) 389700

www.nationaltrust.org.uk

Burial ground of Anglo-Saxon kings with a museum of priceless treasures.

Open: 11am–5pm generally (see website for details).

Tide Mill, Woodbridge (W)

Tide Mill Way

☎ (01728) 746959

www.tidemill.org.uk

Rare example of a nineteenth-century mill.

Open: 11am–5pm Apr Sat & Sun. May–Sep daily.

The central Suffolk area is brimming with attractions and visitors will be spoilt for choice when planning a day out. Ancient and historic sites include the fabulous twelfth-century castle at Framlingham and the area is rich in old windmills and watermills. Nature lovers can enjoy a number of wildlife sites, including the National Nature Reserve at Redgrave and Lopham Fen – one of the last remaining refuges of the enigmatic Fen Raft Spider. There are also manor houses, priory remains and a wartime airfield to be discovered.

Yoxford to Haughley

Alongside the A140, which runs from north to south providing a direct route from Norwich to Ipswich, the A1120 is the main route across central Suffolk. It runs from the A12 turn-off at **Yoxford** in a south-westerly direction towards

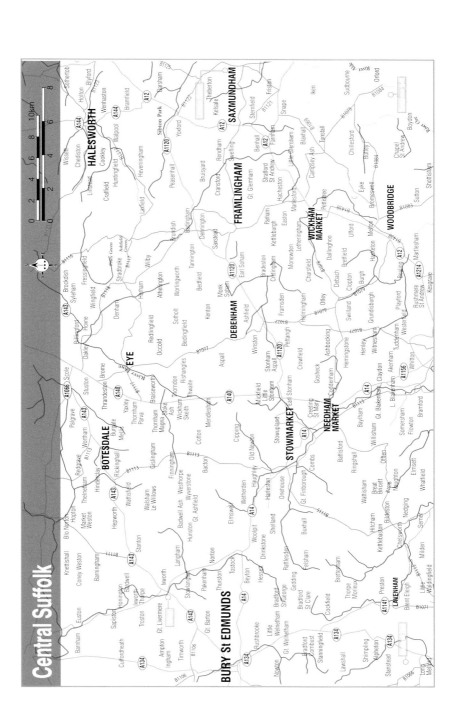

Central Suffolk

the market town of Stowmarket.

Yoxford is a small and attractive village surrounded by the parkland of three country houses in an area known as the 'Garden of Suffolk'. On its outskirts stands **Satis House**, an eighteenth-century building once mentioned by Charles Dickens in *Great Expectations*. It is now a fine restaurant. Along the main street of the village (off the A12) is also the **Griffin Inn**, which began life as a hostelry in the sixteenth century and is believed to have been a regular haunt for smugglers. It is also well worth a visit.

The River Yox, from which the village takes its name, flows through the settlement close to the entrance of **Cockfield Hall**, a sixteenth-century private house that stands in forty acres (16 hectares) of historic parkland. Lady Catherine Grey, the sister of Lady Jane Grey, was imprisoned at Cockfield Hall in 1567, but died shortly after her arrival and was buried in **Yoxford Church**. While the hall is not open to the public, it can be viewed from a footpath that runs along the back of the property.

The A1120 is a meandering route which takes in many picturesque villages. One of the best is **Peasenhall**, which retains the charm of a nineteenth-century hamlet and still has its original grocery store. **Emmett's** has been trading from the site since 1840 and continues to provide some of the finest smoked ham and bacon in the east of England.

Despite its harmonious setting, Peasenhall is often remembered as the scene of a murder mystery. In 1902, servant girl **Rose Harsent** had her throat cut and died in the home of her employer. William Gardiner, a local choirmaster and Sunday school teacher, was tried for the crime, although two separate juries failed to find him guilty. The real murderer was never discovered.

Following the A1120 for a little over 7 miles (11km) brings the traveller to **Saxtead Green**. This is the site of a **Post Mill** and has been since 1287. The present mill has been refurbished and is in excellent working order. Visitors can climb its wooden stairs and watch the mechanism turn on its post to face the wind. It is probably the most visited windmill in Suffolk.

A detour off the A1120 at this point takes travellers on the B1119 to the town of **Framlingham**. The name is taken from the Saxon word 'Freyn-lingham', which means 'settlement of the strangers', a reference to the invasion of the Danes. While recorded as a seventh-century Anglo-Saxon site, much of Framlingham's known history has resulted from its **Castle**. This was built by the powerful **Bigod family** (see feature box on page 21). The present curtain-walled structure dates from that time, although there was once a wooden motte and bailey castle near the site a century earlier. The battlement walk around the monument provides excellent views over the surrounding countryside. The **Lanman Museum** is housed within the castle walls and holds many artefacts relating to the town's past. With some enjoyable walks around the castle site, this is not an attraction to miss and is great for children.

Framlingham benefited greatly from the prosperity generated by its castle and the town is rich in architecture. A stroll around the triangular **Market Hill** reveals buildings of many ages and styles which combine to give the town its unique charm.

Returning to the main A1120, and less than 2 miles (3km) further on from Saxtead Green, is the stunning village of **Earl Soham**. This has many old houses and cottages, a good proportion of which are listed as being of architectural or historical interest. Most of the village is designated a Conservation Area because of its collective historical interest.

A short distance beyond this, visitors can turn south onto the B1077 to find another post mill at **Framsden**. This was rescued from dereliction in the late 1960s. Built in 1760, it was refitted in 1836, when it was raised to its present height of nearly fifty feet (15m) and the substructure enclosed by a two-storey brick roundhouse. Much of its eighteenth-century structure survives today.

Close by are **Helmingham Hall Gardens**, which sit within a Tudor estate of 400 acres (160 hectares). Helmingham Hall was completed in 1510 and is surrounded by a wide moat that is believed to pre-date the house. The attraction features some stunning ornamental gardens, a coach house tearoom and pretty orchard, all with full wheelchair access. It also provides a venue for numerous seasonal exhibitions and events and offers safari rides to see the red and fallow deer and highland cattle on its extensive deer park.

Less than 5 miles (8km) further north on the B1077 is the most central of Suffolk's villages. **Debenham** lies in the heart of the countryside near the source of the River Deben – an impressive, peaceful village which was once a thriving wool centre. Evidence of this trade is all around in the timber-framed merchants' houses dating from the fourteenth century. Named in the Domesday Book of 1086, it was once one of the most populated places in the area and a number of English kings are thought to have held occasional courts there.

The **High Street** is the main thoroughfare through the village, along which can be found many buildings of interest. These include **56 High Street**, the oldest house in Debenham (possibly twelfth century) and originally a raised aisle hall. Further along is **27 High Street**, formerly The Buck, an old coaching inn. At the rear of this building there was once a Tudor theatre. On a track running north-west from the village is a mysterious stone known locally as the Groaning Stone (see feature box on page 50).

A short distance north-west of Debenham is the **Mid-Suffolk Light Railway Museum**, known affectionately as 'The Middy'. This is best accessed along the A140, some 14 miles (23km) north of Ipswich. It is well signposted and is the only railway museum in Suffolk. It is a classic example of a railway built late on in the great railway age that never paid its way and eventually went bust. The atmosphere is of a sleepy country station of the 1930s to 1950s.

Some 7 miles (11km) directly south of the museum, and back onto the main A1120, is **Stonham Barns**, a leisure, shopping and rural pursuits complex.

Suffolk's Standing Stones

Legends about standing stones and the strange powers they embody are commonplace in most parts of Britain. And while Suffolk may have comparatively fewer mysterious stones than other counties, the stories surrounding those that do exist are no less appealing, fascinating and mystifying.

At Bungay, in the north-east of the county, is the **Druid's Stone**, an embedded granite boulder, which stands in the churchyard of St Mary's. Many have claimed that this marks the spot of earlier pagan rituals and stories abound about the running and dancing games that can be performed around the boulder to summon the Devil. In reality, it is more likely to be a direction stone, extracted from the ruins of nearby Bungay Castle.

The **Groaning Stone** at Debenham in central Suffolk is believed to be a direction marker, situated as it is along a track heading west from the north end of the village. Locals claim the stone moves and groans at midnight, with the striking of the church clock. Close to the village of Wattisham, south of Stowmarket, lies another direction marker. At less than three feet (1m) tall, the **Wattisham Stone** sits at the junction of three roads. It is believed to move at the sound of chiming from the bells of the church tower in nearby Bildeston.

The jagged **Preaching Stone** in the town of Mendlesham is held to have been a common rallying point for medieval friars to deliver their sermons, while the **Druid Stone** in the village of Wenhaston is thought to have been a place of pagan worship.

Other stones have equally intriguing stories. The **Devil's Stone** in the nearby village of Middleton is said to have been a meeting point for local witches and a place where Satan's voice could be summoned. Similarly, the **Witches' Stones** in Lowestoft, a collection of small, roughly cemented rocks near to Cart Score, are alleged to have been a regular haunt of two Lowestoft women tried and hanged for witchcraft in 1665. The stones themselves are believed to be weather makers, bringing rain if doused in water.

Some unusual stones mark key events in history. This includes the **Hartest Stone**, a large limestone rock which sits on the village green and is said to have been sited by local men to mark battle victories in the War of the Spanish Succession.

Suffolk may not have a huge volume of mysterious stones across its rural landscape, but those that do exist are worth recognising for the richness and diversity of the tales that surround them.

Debenham

Earl Soham

The barns are open seven days a week and include a nine-hole golf course, fishing lake, horse sanctuary and a wide range of arts and crafts. There is a caravan and camping park close by and an excellent **Birds of Prey & Nature Centre**. Altogether, something to keep all members of the family interested.

At the tail-end of the A1120 on the outskirts of Stowmarket is **Pike's Meadow**, an area of mown grassland along the River Rattlesden. The area is great for informal picnics and games, while younger visitors can make use of the football goals and basketball area. There are a number of old riverside willows on the site and a variety of other trees throughout the area.

Four miles (6km) north-west of Stowmarket, and signposted from the A14, are the gardens and park of **Haughley Park**, a Jacobean manor house. The house itself has a striking red-brick construction dating from 1620, although the north end was rebuilt in a Georgian style around 1820. There are three short woodland walks through old broadleaf and pine woodland with bluebells, lily-of-the-valley, camellias, rhododendrons and azaleas throughout different times of the spring and summer. There is also a walled garden with a rose arbour, vegetables and fruit trees.

The village of **Haughley** itself has a number of rendered and painted houses, some of them thatched. The settlement was important as a market town in the Middle Ages and its duck pond was once part of the moat surrounding a motte and bailey wooden castle – in its time one of the most important in East Anglia.

Wickham Market to Otley

The Georgian and timber-framed houses of **Wickham Market** make this small town particularly appealing. It has a great **Market Square** and some quaint shops. The octagonal tower and lead spire of the town's **All Saints' Church** has been lovingly restored and the seven-hundred-year-old building is very graceful.

Wickham Market sits just off the A12 Ipswich to Lowestoft route, some five miles (8km) north of Woodbridge. A little further north of the town is the **Easton Farm Park**, which is set up to cater for younger visitors. The Farm Park sits on the River Deben in a stunning range of Victorian farm buildings. The activities available include pony, cart and train rides, an adventure playground, pedal tractors and go-karts and an indoor soft play area. There is also a Riverside Cafe offering home-made lunches and snacks.

North-east of this is **Parham Airfield**, which is home to the **390th Bomb Group Memorial Museum**, housed in a restored control tower. Admission to the museum is free and the museum holds a lot of fascinating World War II history.

Four miles (6km) north-west of Wickham Market is another historic site, this one dating back as far as the twelfth century. The small church of **St Mary's** sits behind a farmyard and contains the remains of **Letheringham Priory**. This was founded around 1194 as a cell to the priory of Ipswich. The brick gatehouse dates from the late fifteenth century and can be found

Bartholomew Gosnold – Explorer

Bartholomew Gosnold (1571–1607) voyaged to the New World, where in 1602 he discovered Cape Cod and Martha's Vineyard, which he named after his infant daughter. In 1607, thirteen years before the Mayflower landed, he returned to found Jamestown colony in Virginia, the first permanent English-speaking settlement in America. It is said that the two voyages were planned at the hearthside of Otley Hall.

Gosnold recruited Captain John Smith to lead the second voyage. Smith was rescued from death by Pocahontas, the beautiful daughter of Indian Chief Powhatan. The voyage was also to have a significant impact on the literary world – William Shakespeare's final play *The Tempest* was inspired by reports of the voyage.

behind Abbey Farm.

A journey of some 8 miles (13km) west along the B1078 from Wickham Market will bring visitors to the B1079 turn-off to **Otley.** The village is home to **Otley Hall**, a privately-owned, grade I listed house, which has a long history and is situated in ten acres of gardens. The sixteenth-century moated manor house was home to the Gosnold family for over 300 years. The house is open all year for private tours of the house and gardens by appointment. In addition, there are usually a number of public open days, with guided tours and themed entertainment events.

Hoxne to Pakenham

The attractive village of **Hoxne** sits close to the border with Norfolk along the top edge of central Suffolk, close to Billingford and around four miles (6km) east of Diss. It is reputed to be the place where **Edmund, King of East Anglia**, was captured and slain by the Vikings in AD869 (see feature box on page 80). A memorial near the village marks the spot where the unfortunate king is believed to have died.

Hoxne was also the site of a significant **Roman hoard** which was discovered in 1992. A local man searching for a lost hammer in a nearby field uncovered around 15,000 Roman coins and other priceless artefacts buried in a chest. The hoard is now on display at the British Museum. Hoxne is a pretty village with some characteristically picture-box Suffolk homes. One of the oldest buildings along its main street is **The Swan**, a public house that serves great food and drink.

The A143 rejoins Suffolk from Norfolk close to Hoxne and continues south-west towards Bury St Edmunds (most of the earlier route from Bungay is in Norfolk). The route passes through an area rich in nature trusts, including **Market Weston Fen, Mellis Common, Thelnetham Fen** and **Wortham Ling**.

The area also boasts the **National Nature Reserve of Redgrave and Lopham Fen**, which spans the two counties. It is the largest remaining river

Peasenhall Village

Hoxne

valley fen in England and, as one of the most important wetlands in Europe, has international protection. As well as open fen, the reserve includes a mixture of wet heathland, open water, scrub and woodland. The underlying acid and alkaline geology has resulted in characteristic wildlife, including many species now rare in Britain, such as the fen raft spider, butterwort and marsh fragrant orchid. Not far off is the **Knettishall Country Park** with 400 hundred acres of breckland, heath and woodland.

The A143 route is also within easy travelling distance of a number of wind and watermills that tell much about Suffolk's agricultural and industrial past. **Thelnetham Tower Mill**, which is to the west of Redgrave, was built in 1819 and worked until the early 1920s. It has two pairs of wind-driven millstones. **Stanton Post Mill**, some 5 miles (8km) away and closer to Bury St Edmunds, is still in full working

order, producing flour by wind power. It dates from 1751 and was restored in the 1980s.

In comparison, **Bardwell Tower Mill**, only a couple of miles (3km) west of Stanton, is still in the process of being restored and is currently without its sails. The mill was built in the 1820s and can be found in the village centre. A similar short journey north-west will reveal **Euston Watermill**, a small estate mill in an attractive setting on the edge of **Euston Park**. It powered a pump to raise water to a tank in its church-like tower and is believed to date from the 1730s.

Euston Hall itself was once a manor belonging to the Abbey at Bury St Edmunds and has been the home of the Dukes of Grafton for over 300 years. It has been open to the public during the summer for over twenty-five years and contains a fine collection of paintings by Van Dyck and Stubbs. The park and river layout of the estate was designed by **William Kent** and the project was completed by **Capability Brown**.

Closer still to Bury St Edmunds are **Pakenham Tower Mill** and **Pakenham Watermill**. The tower mill is one of Suffolk's best-known windmills and began life around 1830. It was in use until the 1950s and repaired in 2000. The watermill worked commercially until 1974, after which it was bought and restored. Dating from 1814, it sits on the site of a much older Tudor mill. Stoneground flour is still made at the mill and is available for sale.

Standing on a hill overlooking the village of Pakenham is **St Mary's Parish Church,** which has an attractive octagonal tower set centrally on the crossing of its nave and transepts. It contains some fine wooden wall plaques and stained-glass windows.

Walpole to Eye

The B1117 road from Halesworth, ten miles (16km) west of Southwold, to the junction with the A140 is another well-travelled route through central Suffolk. This takes in the attractive village of **Walpole**, which houses one of the most important nonconformist buildings in Britain. **Walpole Old Chapel** looks like an old Suffolk farmhouse with a few gravestones, but contains the original pulpit, box pews and galleries of the chapel. It was in use during the turmoil of the English Civil War.

A little further on is the site of **Heveningham Hall**, the biggest and grandest stately home in Suffolk. This was built for the Dutchman **Gerard Vanneck** in the late eighteenth century.

Robert Taylor was the architect and Capability Brown laid out the parkland in which the house sits. Despite falling into disrepair during an inheritance dispute in the 1980s, it has now been restored and retains one of England's stateliest and longest Georgian frontages. While the hall is not open to the public, its grounds are open to the public during the annual **Heveningham Country Fair** in July.

Three miles (5km) beyond this is the charming village of **Laxfield**. No fewer than forty-eight of its thatched and timber-framed buildings are listed as being of historic and architectural interest. Not to be missed is the **King's Head** public house, known locally as the 'The Low House', a fifteenth-century thatched alehouse with high-backed settles, great beer and fantastic food.

The **Guild Hall of St Mary**, situated in the main street opposite

Framlingham Castle

the church, is particularly noteworthy. This was donated to the village by the Lord of the Manor as a church house in 1461 and now serves as the **Laxfield Museum**. Access to the museum is gained by some steep winding stairs to the first floor. It contains exhibits relating to local rural, domestic and working life from the nineteenth century onwards.

Laxfield was the birthplace of Puritan **William Dowsing**, who was responsible for destroying and defacing religious objects and icons in over 150 churches across Suffolk during 1643 and 1644. By luck or design, the sacramental font in the fifteenth-century parish church of **All Saints** has survived to this day.

A dozen miles on from Laxfield is the significant town of Eye. This derives its name from the Old English word for 'island', suggesting that the settlement was once surrounded by water marshes. By the time of the Norman Conquest, Eye was already an important and wealthy town. However, its economic and military importance waned from 1173 following an attack on **Eye Castle** by Hugh Bigod, during the rebellion against Henry II (see feature box on page 21). The ruins of the castle keep are open to visitors and the elliptical shape of the former outer bailey can still be traced along **Castle Street** and **Church Street**.

The fourteenth-century **Church of St Peter and St Paul** in Eye is one of the best in Suffolk and has some beautiful flushwork on its tower and a superb fifteenth-century rood screen (originating from the Great Massingham Priory of Norfolk). Other attractions include the **Guildhall** (now a private house)

and the **Town Hall**, which dates from 1856. Elsewhere, Eye has around 160 listed buildings.

Amenities in and around the town include **The Pennings,** a picnic site beside the River Dove, and the **Town**

William Dowsing (1596–1668)

William Dowsing was an English iconoclast who operated at the time of the English Civil War. He became Provost-Marshall of the Puritan armies of the Eastern Association (covering the eastern counties), responsible for supplies and administration.

In 1643 he was appointed by the Captain-General of the Eastern Association, the Earl of Manchester, as 'Commissioner for the Destruction of Monuments of Idolatry and Superstition', to remove and abolish all symbols of superstition and idolatry, including fixed altars, chancel steps, crucifixes, images of the Virgin Mary and pictures of saints or superstitious inscriptions.

Dowsing visited over 250 churches in East Anglia, removing or defacing items he believed to be idolatrous. He used assistants or local labourers to carry out his work and backed this up with military force where required. Each church was charged a noble (a third of a pound) for his services. When Manchester, his patron, fell out with Oliver Cromwell in late 1644, Dowsing's commission ceased.

Moors Recreation Site, which has play areas, pitches and a large area of woodland walks. The **Queens Head** public house, behind the Town Hall, is an original town hostelry and retains its centuries-old charm.

Despite having fewer than 2,000 inhabitants, the town has its own annual **Eye Show & Country Fair** at Goodrich Park in nearby Palgrave. The event regularly attracts around 50,000 visitors and includes aeronautical displays, military bands, steam engines, horse shows, flower stands and a host of trade and shopping facilities.

Some 3 miles (5km) away from Eye, just off the A140, is the 2,000-acre (800-hectare) **Thornham Estate.** Activities here include a field study centre, walks and a walled garden, which is a horticultural therapy centre.

Walks in the Area

As elsewhere in the county, there is an extensive network of footpaths and tracks criss-crossing the landscape of central Suffolk. These provide walking opportunities for all ages and abilities.

There are waymarked circular routes of between 3 to 7 miles (5–11km) around a number of towns and villages in the area, including Debenham, Framlingham and Peasenhall.

Eye also has its own popular 'town trail' and the nearby Thornham Walks provide 12 miles (19km) of waymarked trails around the Thornham Estate. One part of the facilities includes a surfaced path, suitable for both pushchairs and wheelchairs, leading for half a mile (1km) to the Thornham Walled Garden. This takes walkers along the Thornham Rock Trail to a Victorian folly. Walks'

staff are also available to lead and organise guided walks and environmental activities for groups, including some popular environmental birthday parties. The Walks are open each day from 9.00am to 6.00pm. Dogs on leads are also welcome.

One of the most popular walking routes in the area is the Mid Suffolk Footpath – a long-distance route from Stowmarket to Hoxne. This begins at the Green's Meadow picnic site and stretches for over 20 miles (32km) through the heart of the county, taking in Mendlesham and Eye.

The local Tourist Information Centres can provide route maps for all of the walks mentioned above.

Cycle Rides

The principal cycle ride through central Suffolk is the Heart of Suffolk Cycle Route, which covers a distance of 78 miles (125 km) across the gently rolling landscape and through the pretty villages and old market towns of the area. Fully signed in both directions it takes in Eye, Debenham and Framlingham before connecting to other parts of the county.

Central Suffolk also forms part of The National Byway, a 4,000-mile (6,436 km), signposted, leisure cycle route around Britain on quiet country roads, lanes and tracks. In the East of England, the route currently runs from Ipswich, dividing into two directions. One of these goes via central Suffolk to Bury St Edmunds, then onto The Fens to the south of Peterborough.

Parts of the area, mainly around Framlingham, also fall within the North Sea Cycle Route mentioned in Chapter

Eye Castle

1 (see www.northsea-cycle.com).

Details of more localised cycle rides can be obtained from any of the Tourist Information Centres in Suffolk.

Car Tours

This chapter has set out the principal sites and attractions in central Suffolk on the basis of the main car routes through the area. Further short car tours can be planned around these main routes to discover other highlights of the central Suffolk countryside.

Public Transport

Public transport in the central Suffolk area includes rail, buses and community transport. Both the East Suffolk and Ipswich to Norwich main lines run through parts of the area. The closest stations on the East Suffolk line are those at Wickham Market, Darsham

Eye

Framlingham

and Halesworth. Nearby stations on the Ipswich to Norwich line are those at Needham Market and Stowmarket. There is also a junction on this line to Bury St Edmunds with stops at Elmswell and Thurston – both of which fall within the western fringe of

Eye

central Suffolk.

The local bus network is good and most major towns and villages are well served. As mentioned in Chapters 1 & 2, a community transport scheme also operates across rural areas like central Suffolk. The Suffolk County Council Customer Service Centre can provide you with further information on ☎ (0845) 606 6067.

Debenham

Places To Visit

(W) = Suggestions for wet days

(C) = Good entertainment value for children

Easton Farm Park (C)

Easton, near Woodbridge, IP13 0EQ

☎ (01728) 746457

www.eastonfarmpark.co.uk

Award-winning farm park in the Deben River valley. Children can meet and feed the animals. Includes adventure play areas, cafe and gift shop.

Open: 10.30am–4pm Feb. 10.30am–6pm Mar–Sep. 10.30am–4pm Oct.

Euston Hall (W)

Twelve miles north of Bury St Edmunds on the A1088

☎ (01842) 766366

www.eustonhall.co.uk

The hall contains a unique collection of paintings of the court of Charles II.

Open: Varies (see website for details).

Eye Castle (C)

Castle Street, Eye, IP23 7AW

☎ (01449) 676800

A Norman motte and bailey castle with medieval walls and a Victorian folly. Excellent panorama of the town of Eye.

Open: 9am–dusk daily Easter–Oct.

Framlingham Castle (C)

Castle Street, Framlingham, IP13 9BP

☎ (01728) 724189

Magnificent twelfth-century baronial fortress with battlement walks and stunning views.

Open: 10am–6pm daily Apr–Sep. 10am–4pm Oct–Mar Thu–Mon.

Helmingham Hall Gardens

On B1077, 9 miles (14km) north of Ipswich

☎ (01473) 890799

www.helmingham.com

Gardens surrounding a moated, grade I listed, Tudor Hall. Includes a shop, tearoom and local produce.

Open: 2pm–6pm May–Sep Wed & Sun.

Mid-Suffolk Light Railway Museum (C)

Brockford Station, Wetheringsett, IP14 5PW

☎ (01449) 766899

www.mslr.org.uk

A re-created light railway station with exhibitions.

Open: 11am–5pm Easter–Sep Sun & BHs. 1pm–5pm Aug Wed.

Saxstead Green Post Mill

Nineteenth-century post mill with roundhouse.

Open: 12pm–5pm Apr–Sep Fri, Sat & BHs.

Stonham Barns (W) (C)

Pettaugh Road, Stonham Aspal,
IP14 6A

☎ (01449) 711755

www.stonhambarns.co.uk

Specialist shops, owl sanctuary, nine-hole golf course, fishing lakes, caravan park, garden centre, restaurant and coffee shop.

Open: 10am–5pm Mon–Sat. 10am–4pm Sun all year round.

South Suffolk

Extending up from the Shotley Peninsula, the south Suffolk area takes in the valleys of the rivers Box, Brett and Glem and the historic towns of Hadleigh and Sudbury. Many of its towns and villages are nationally known for a variety of reasons: Kersey for its picture-postcard beauty; Polstead for its magnificent black cherries and for the *Murder in the Red Barn* of Maria Marten; Stoke by-Nayland for its magnificent church and golf club; Lavenham for its wealth of medieval buildings; and Long Melford for its antique shops and the historic sites of Kentwell Hall and Melford Hall. All of this sits within a landscape of stunning beauty and with over 4,000 buildings listed as being of architectural or historic interest, south Suffolk has much to boast about.

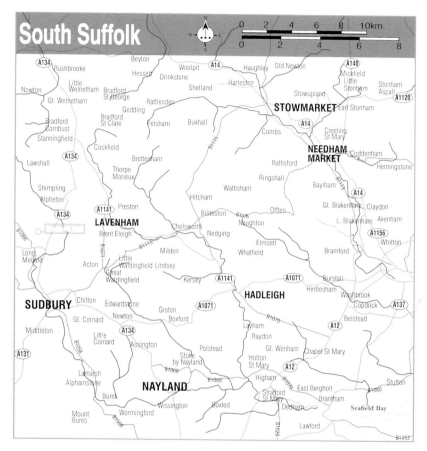

Ipswich to Bures

The A1071 is the main road from Ipswich to the market town of Hadleigh. The route winds through some rolling countryside and passes a number of attractive rural villages. North of the stretch just outside of Ipswich is **Burstall**, which has some pretty houses, a fascinating arts & crafts-style **village hall** and the fourteenth-century church of **St Mary**. The latter contains an interesting rood screen dado and an impressive stained-glass memorial window, commemorating those who died in World War I.

Hintlesham is the first significant settlement along the route, marked as it is by the sharp bends of the road which circumnavigate the local manor house. **Hintlesham Hall** is one of the best hotels in Suffolk, superbly situated in over 175 acres (70 hectares) of the south Suffolk countryside. It is a beautiful Elizabethan building, steeped in history, with a wide range of facilities, including an eighteen-hole golf course.

Further south is one of Suffolk's truly hidden gems. The tiny village of **Little Wenham** contains the parish church of **All Saints**, which has some of the earliest and best wall paintings in the county and some pre-Reformation brasses. Close by is **Little Wenham Hall**, a thirteenth-century L-shaped brick and flint block, which once stood against a timber-framed hall. Founded by the de Holebroke family, it is one of the earliest examples of the use of brickwork in England, dating back to 1275. While the site is strictly private, with no public access, it can be viewed from the church and a nearby public footpath.

Hadleigh is the major town in this part of south Suffolk. It was once a royal settlement in which the ninth-century Viking King Guthrum is said to be buried. Its prosperity came as a result of its connections with the wool trade. Indeed the architecture of many of the houses along its **High Street** hint at its once considerable wealth. Most are well preserved, colour-washed in yellow, white or Suffolk pink and occasionally decorated with elaborate pargeting.

The spire of the parish church of **St Mary's** dominates the skyline of the town. This stands beside the impressive red-bricked **Deanery Tower** which was built in 1495. In the same area are some medieval buildings which include the **Guildhall** and **Town Hall**.

As a thriving market town, Hadleigh has some good amenities, including a swimming pool and leisure centre and a wide range of shops. Nearby, and just off the A1071, is the RSPB reserve of **Wolves Wood**. This is an ancient wood containing forty-six ponds. The reserve is open all year round and has parking facilities. It is great for sightings of garden warblers, marsh tits and nightingales.

South-west of Hadleigh is the pretty village of Polstead, which sits on the River Box. It derives its name from the ponds which lie at the bottom of a steep hill leading up to the village green on one side with **St Mary's church** and **Polstead Hall** on the other side. **Polstead Heath** is the site of a nineteenth-century orchard and is famous for its cherries.

The village has two good pubs, a farm shop and a caravan touring park. The area is popular with walkers and local paths are both well signed and maintained. Polstead also has one other claim to fame – it was the setting for the **Murder in the**

Pargeting

English plasterwork became increasingly elaborate in the sixteenth century. Some of the most opulent ornamental plastering, or pargeting, was produced over the next 150 years with a high point around 1660 (a good example being Ancient House in Ipswich), after which the technique began to fall out of fashion.

Alongside its neighbouring counties in the East, Suffolk is the traditional home of pargeting, although documented examples can be found as far away as York and the West Country.

Red Barn, one of the most legendary murder mysteries in nineteenth-century England.

Further south is **Stoke-by-Nayland**, whose landscape is dominated by the magnificent 120-foot (36m) high tower of the church of **St Mary**. This one was a favourite of artist John Constable (see feature box on page 40) and appears in many of his landscapes (although not always in the right place!). The village has a number of fine timber-framed buildings and a sixteenth-century **Guildhall** now converted into three homes. It also has a large **golf club** which sits within 300 acres (120 hectares) of undulating countryside, designated as an Area of Outstanding Natural Beauty.

Kersey, just over 2 miles (3km) north-west of Hadleigh, is another beautiful village and one of the most photographed in the county. Its main street runs down from the hill on which its fifteenth-century church stands to a shallow ford at its bottom. The buildings of the remainder of the street then stretch up a hill the other side of the valley, making the whole scene timeless and picturesque. Painted weavers' cottages sit snugly alongside the **Bell Inn** in this quintessentially Suffolk village.

Further along the A1071 is **Boxford**, home of some large fruit orchards and more timber-framed buildings. **Groton**, to its north, is well-known for its links with the **Pilgrim Fathers**, who colonised the New England states of America in the early seventeenth century. John Winthrop, of **Groton Hall**, emigrated in 1630 to take charge of the Massachusetts Company. He founded the city of Boston and became the first governor of the State.

Eight miles (13km) south-west of Groton are Bures St Mary and Bures

The Murder in the Red Barn

The Murder in the Red Barn has passed into legend. The story of Maria Marten's death has all the popular elements of melodrama, including a wicked local squire, an innocent village maiden and a mother's mysterious dream in which the murder was discovered. But the tale is more than a legend. Maria Marten was murdered in The Red Barn at Polstead. Her lover, William Corder, was arrested for the murder, brought to trial and executed at Bury St Edmunds in August 1828. So much is historical fact, but even before the trial the elements of this sordid country crime were being sensationalised by media hype. As the nineteenth century progressed new elements were grafted onto the story and fact and fiction merged into a folk tale which still fascinates today.

Hamlet, known collectively as **Bures**. This historic area, which has around fifty listed buildings, has many attractions. Alongside the mill, lock and maltings of its agricultural and industrial past, Bures has a thirteenth-century chapel dedicated to **St Stephen** and a magnificent moated Elizabethan house known as **Smallbridge Hall**. This was constructed in 1555 and played host to Queen Elizabeth I in both 1561 and 1579.

The area surrounding the village is rich in natural habitats, including some **water meadows** and the **Arger Fen**, a small fragment of a wildwood that once covered Suffolk over a thousand years ago. There are several walks through the area which is designated as a Site of Special Scientific Interest. It is one of only two woods in eastern England to have a large number of wild cherry trees.

Sudbury to Needham Market

Sudbury is a thriving and ancient market town set in the heart of the River Stour valley and is well known as the home of artist **Thomas Gainsborough**, whose statue stands in front of **St Stephen's**, the main church of the town. The town existed in Anglo-Saxon times and became a major centre for the weaving industry from the thirteenth century. Prominent among its varied architecture are rows of typical three-storey **weavers' houses**.

Sudbury has three fine **medieval churches** and some impressive timber-framed cloth **merchants' houses**. The **Town Hall** dates from 1826 and **The Quay** area of the town includes the remnants of its days as a busy port – one old warehouse has been converted into the **Quay Theatre**.

Other interesting buildings include the **Corn Exchange** (now the town's library), built in 1841, with its four giant Tuscan columns, and **Gainsborough's House**, which dates from 1500 and retains many interesting features. Its Georgian facade, built by the artist's father, and other elegant additions are eighteenth century. The house is now a museum complete with more of the artist's paintings, drawings and prints than anywhere else in the world.

The main shopping area of the town is centred on **Market Hill**. On Thursdays and Saturdays the area is crowded with stalls for the long-established markets, which are popular with locals and tourists. Shopping is good in Sudbury and there is ample free parking close to the town centre, including some parking spaces for disabled people on Market Hill and on Gainsborough Street.

Thomas Gainsborough – Suffolk Artist

Thomas Gainsborough was one of the most famous portrait and landscape painters in eighteenth-century Britain. He was born in Sudbury, where his father was a weaver involved with the wool trade. At the age of thirteen he so impressed his father with his drawing skills that he was allowed to go to London to study art in 1740. Here he trained as an engraver, before eventually becoming associated with William Hogarth and his school.

Gainsborough's keen observation of nature and people is reflected in his paintings, a style which once caused John Constable to say that, 'On looking at them, we find tears in our eyes and know not what brings them.' Gainsborough himself was more direct when he said, 'I'm sick of portraits, and wish very much to . . . walk off to some sweet village, where I can paint landskips (sic) and enjoy the fag end of life in quietness and ease.' He died of cancer on 2 August 1788.

Deanery Tower and St Mary's Church, Hadleigh

Guildhall, Hadleigh

The town also has some good public houses and restaurants and a **Heritage Centre & Museum** behind the Town Hall. This tells the story of Sudbury's early connections with royalty, Simon of Sudbury, Gainsborough and the silk industry.

Visiting families can also explore **Belle Vue Park**, which lies only a few minutes' walk from Market Hill. This has beautiful lawns and floral displays, as well as aviaries and other collections of animals. For the more active there are public tennis courts and a skateboarding area. There is also a **Leisure Centre** on Station Road, complete with a swimming pool, beach area, flume and wave machine. Elsewhere there is also a **Ten Pin Bowling Alley** and **Indoor Adventure Playground** for younger children.

Sudbury is well served by its rail connection and has good road links. For nature lovers, the area has a wide range of local beauty spots, including **The Croft, Valley Walk** and **King's Meadow**. Nearby is also the **Great Cornard Country Park**, a large area with a picnic site and walks overlooking the Stour Valley.

The B1115 route out of Sudbury takes travellers through the delightful villages of **Monks Eleigh** and **Chelsworth**. Both could claim to be the picture of a rural idyll. Monks Eleigh is on the northern bank of the River Brett with a village green bordered by colour-washed houses, on which sits a fascinating old water pump. Curiously it has no real connections to any monks and has never been the site of a monastery. It has a recently established **Millennium Green** which sits within the village's conservation area.

The style and beauty of Chelsworth has been admired for many years. The writer Julian Tennyson once described it as his favourite Suffolk village. There are sixty or so houses which line this mile-long stretch of the B1115. Each has its own attractions and adornments and contributes to the overall splendour of this pretty hamlet. One of the seasonal highlights of the village is its celebrated **Open Gardens Day**.

A little south of both villages is the small hamlet of **Milden**, which sits high above the Brett Valley. The towerless church of **St Peter** is worth stopping for and on the edge of the village is **Milden Hall**, a listed sixteenth-century farmhouse with a large Tudor barn surrounded by ancient wildflower meadows. While not open to the public, the hall offers bed & breakfast and self-catering accommodation and provides a wide range of activities for families interested in conservation and environmental stewardship.

Bildeston, just north of the junction of the B1115 and B1078, is another village made rich by the wool trade. It was once famed for its manufacture of good-quality blankets. Like so many of the communities in this area, it too has a church called **St Mary's**. It also has some characteristic and appealing timber-framed houses, many of which stand at interesting angles.

Just off the B1078 towards Needham Market, lovers of military history can visit the **Wattisham Airfield Museum**. This is open between April and October and contains the history of the airfield, in photographs and memorabilia, within the old station chapel. During World War II, the airfield buzzed with the sound of British medium-range bombers and later became a central supply depot for the American 8th Air Force.

Some 9 miles (14km) east of Wattisham is an attraction of a very different kind. The

Baylham House Rare Breeds Farm is off the B1113 between Needham Market and Great Blakenham. It is a working livestock farm with breeding animals to feed, picnic areas and both riverside and lakeside walks. A visitor centre also provides souvenirs, cream teas, light lunches and other refreshments.

Needham Market, further along the B1078, has one main **High Street**, on which can be found a number of Georgian houses, colour-washed cottages and quaint shops. The market charter of the town was granted by Henry III in 1245 and helped the settlement to flourish. Much of its later prosperity came through the wool trade, although it was wool combing, rather than weaving, that became its staple trade.

The modern buildings on both sides of the High Street around the car park bear witness to the bombing of the town by German aircraft during World War II. This destroyed several properties, including the telephone exchange, and damaged many more.

Some of the attractions in the town include the **Victorian Railway Station** (built in 1849), **Town Hall** (opened in 1866) and **Almshouses** (complete with medieval carvings). **Tudor House** is a fine timber-framed building that typifies the many fifteenth- and sixteenth-century houses that lie behind the brick facades of the High Street.

Needham Market has a good rail link and sits just off the main A14 route from Ipswich to Bury St Edmunds. On its outskirts is the popular **Needham Lake** site, which attracts sizeable numbers of visitors. It has a variety of wildlife and a surfaced lakeside path to take visitors around the former gravel pit. Part of the site is a Local Nature Reserve with a wetland area, meadows and woodland. Wild flowers are plentiful with pyramidal and bee orchids easily seen from the paths.

The site includes picnic areas, play equipment for children and plenty of grass for games. During the school holidays there are also regular children's activities and storytelling events. Anglers can also use the site and day permits can be purchased in the town.

Long Melford to Stowmarket

Long Melford, 3 miles (5km) north of Sudbury, is set along a broad, tree-lined street and fully deserves its name. Its main thoroughfare is over a mile long – running from its great green southwards besides the River Chad – and contains an appealing range of eighteenth- and nineteenth-century-fronted shops and houses. With some evidence of earlier Roman settlement, Long Melford was another medieval village to prosper as a result of the wool trade. Since Tudor times it has been a busy and bustling village, attracting visitors from all over the world.

The green dominates the west end of the main street. Close by are three of its jewels. **Holy Trinity Church** provides a magnificent view down over the green. It is arguably the finest church in East Anglia, with almost cathedral-like proportions, and dates from the fifteenth century. Among its many attractions are the massive tower, a clerestory roof, original medieval glass and superlative brass rubbings.

The Elizabethan **Kentwell Hall**, situated at the northern end of the village, is a moated mansion dating from 1500. The house and gardens are open to the public

Statue of Thomas Gainsborough outside St Peter's Church, Sudbury

and the venue holds a number of historic recreations each year with excellent use of re-enactors – people dressed in Tudor clothes, speaking and engaging in a wide range of sixteenth-century activities. The site also includes a working farm with rare breeds, stunning gardens and a wide range of original Tudor crafts.

Just below the church on the far side of the green sits **Melford Hall**, another Elizabethan mansion with turrets, an octagonal summer house and an imposing gatehouse. This is owned by the National Trust and has been the home of the Hyde Parker family since 1786. **Beatrix Potter** was a cousin of the family and the house contains a collection of memorabilia devoted to her. The house has a classic Tudor interior and

Monks Eleigh

a fine panelled banqueting hall. Elizabeth I was once entertained lavishly here, along with 2,000 members of her court.

Long Melford is a shopper's heaven. Its main street contains several antique shops, art galleries, designer boutiques and gift shops, alongside a wide variety of restaurants, teashops, cafes, pubs and hotels. There is also ample free parking, allowing visitors time to browse and wander at leisure.

Seasonal events in the village include a **Street Fair** in July and **Open Air Con-**

Stowmarket

certs on the green in the summer. The best attended event annually is **The Big Night Out** – East Anglia's largest Guy Fawkes firework display and funfair.

The village of **Lavenham** lies some 5 miles (8km) from Long Melford and was once a major town. Its name appears to have originated from the Saxon for 'Lafa's home' and, as well as Saxon and Norman remains, there is evidence that the settlement was once an important Roman stronghold in an area inhabited by a native British tribe. Lavenham is, without doubt, one of the best-preserved Tudor towns in England, its streets of timber-framed houses paying testament to a time when it was the fourteenth richest town in the country.

The town's great wealth came from a thriving industry in cloth production, which reached its peak in the early sixteenth century. Only a generation later, its economic success waned, leaving Lavenham as a backwater whose inhabitants could not afford to rebuild their homes. Only with the coming of the railways did the village regain its affluence.

There are some fascinating buildings to see in Lavenham. The **Market Place** is a must, with its attractive **Market Cross** – bequeathed to the town in 1500 – and two of the most impressive historic houses. The **Guildhall of Corpus Christi** was built around 1530 and is one of four original guildhalls. Alongside its religious guild activities, the building has served as a prison, workhouse, almshouse, wool store, nursery school, restaurant and 'Welcome Club' for American servicemen in World War II. It now houses a **local museum**, gift shop and tearoom.

The **Little Hall** was built in the 1390s as a family house and workplace. It is now the home of the Suffolk Preservation Society and is open to visitors.

The parish church of **St Peter and St Paul** at the other end of the village is no less grand. Built on the site of an earlier church, most of its present structure is of late perpendicular style and dates from between 1486 and 1525. Its construction was financed mainly through the contributions of several rich Lavenham clothiers.

Though a major tourist attraction, Lavenham is still a working community with free car parking, good shops, galleries, public houses, restaurants and hotels. The **Swan Hotel** on the High Street is an excellent fourteenth-century hotel which offers great food, as do the **Angel Hotel** and **Great House** on the Market Place.

The area to the north of Lavenham is home to some pretty nature reserves and woodland environments. These include **Bull's Wood** at Cockfield and **Bradfield Woods** near Bradfield St Clare. Bull's Wood is an ancient woodland tract that was referred to in the Hundred Rolls of 1279. April is the best month to visit and the wood is famed for its oxlips – delicate yellow-flowered plants which are limited to 100 sites in East Anglia – which carpet parts of the woodland floor in spring. Early-purple orchids are also abundant here and the local birdlife includes chiffchaffs, treecreepers and tawny owls.

Further north, Bradfield Woods is a National Nature Reserve and one of the country's best woodland wildlife sites. The revival of traditional crafts like charcoal production and hurdle making has ensured that it remains a marvellous magnet for wildlife. There is a car park at the reserve entrance and a visitor centre.

Some 8 miles (13km) north-east of Bradfield Woods is the small settlement of **Drinkstone,** which sits alongside the River Blackbourn. The parish church of **All Saints** contains a beautiful rood screen, a scattering of medieval glass and an unusual late-seventeenth-century red-brick tower.

The area also has **two surviving wind-mills** as well as a miller's cottage and a range of traditional outbuildings. Together they tell the story of milling in this area over four centuries. The post mill is one of England's oldest, and the carved date of 1689 inside the building probably refers to a rebuilding, for many of its timbers are much older. The mill was occasionally used as late as 1970.

Nearby **Woolpit** has been a thriving settlement since the first century. The village is famous for the story, documented in the fourteenth century, of two **green children** who were said to have appeared from nowhere. The twelfth-century flint and stone church of **St Mary** has a 140-foot (40m) steeple and dominates the village centre. The other main attraction is the **Woolpit and District Museum,** a seventeenth-century timber-framed building on The Street, with displays of brick making and other features of village life.

The town of **Stowmarket** lies just 7 miles (11km) south-east of Woolpit on the River Gipping. It is easily accessible, being just off the A14 corridor and midway between the larger towns of Ipswich and Bury St Edmunds. It is also served by the main Norwich to Ipswich rail line.

The medieval heart of Stowmarket is based around the 600-year-old parish church of **St Peter and St Mary** and in the area leading down to the riverbank. The town has over 130 listed buildings, the church being classified as of exceptional interest. Its period of industrial growth

The Green Children of Woolpit

In the twelfth century, at the time of King Stephen, two children, a boy and a girl, are said to have appeared in a field one harvest time. They were completely green, from head to foot, and wearing green clothes to match. Some harvesters spotted the pair and took them into the village. While they were offered food, both children initially refused to eat. Luckily some beans had recently been harvested, and the children grabbed the stalks, but finding no pith inside they cried. A man opened a pod and offered them the pith, which they took. The children fed on this until they got used to bread.

Gradually the children changed from green to a more normal colour and learned to speak the language of the village. Over time, they explained that they came from the 'Land of Saint Martin', but could not explain where this was or how they came to be in Woolpit. They said that in their land there were churches, and that another land could be seen over a river; also that the sun did not rise very high. All they could remember was that they were watching their father's herds in the fields when they heard bells, and afterwards found themselves in Woolpit. Later, the boy died of an illness, but the girl married a man from King's Lynn.

began with the opening of its canal in 1793. This brought in new trade and opened up fresh markets to agriculture producers. In particular, the town became noted for its malting industry. Edward III granted the town a market charter in July 1347. Today, the market continues to operate every Thursday and Saturday, offering a wide range of local produce.

Kersey

One of Stowmarket's key attractions is the **Museum of East Anglian Life**, which occupies a seventy-acre site close to the marketplace. It is one of the country's major open-air museums and provides an excellent day out for families. The museum offers wonderful walks by the river, with views of the fully-functioning **Alton Watermill** (carefully dismantled and moved to the site in 1973) and the **Eastbridge Windmill** (a smock drainage mill which originally stood on the Suffolk coast). Elsewhere, there are shady places with picnic tables and a wooden adventure playground for children. There are also working steam engine exhibits and a resident charcoal burner who is happy to explain his rural craft to visitors in his fully-operative forge.

Stowmarket has something for people of all ages. As well as a number of walks in and around the town there is a skate park and an eighteen-hole **golf course** which the English Golf Union has designated as a 'Centre of Excellence'. The town also has a good social scene with the **Regal Theatre**, nightclubs, restaurants and public houses.

Chelsworth

Outside of the town there are picnic spots at a number of sites, the best of which is **Church Meadow**, a Local Nature Reserve lying close to St Mary's Church, Combs. The meadows support a variety of wildlife and wildflowers, including southern marsh orchids. Visitors are welcome, although dogs must be kept on leads as there are often grazing animals present.

Walks in the Area

The picturesque villages, medieval towns and glorious rural landscapes all combine to make south Suffolk an area which many visitors are keen to savour at a gentle pace.

Most of the major towns and villages have their own 'town trails' and circular walks of up to 3 miles (5km) in length. These include Hadleigh, Sudbury, Needham Market, Lavenham and Stowmarket.

There are also some longer walks which take in a number of the sites featured in this chapter. A couple of the best are:

1. The Gipping Valley Path

A signed 17-mile (27km) path from Stowmarket to Ipswich along the old towpath of the River Gipping canal and taking in Needham Market.

2. The Middy Railway Footpath

A walk for railway enthusiasts as well as keen walkers. This follows the route of the old Mid-Suffolk Railway, starting from a silo building in Haughley and concluding at the Mid-Suffolk Light Railway Museum in Wetheringsett.

Route maps for all of these can be obtained from Tourist Information Centres.

Cycle Rides

South Suffolk also offers some excellent cycling country, although it is not quite as flat as newcomers to the area often imagine. There is a signposted Millennium network of South Suffolk Cycle Routes covering some 100 miles (160km). Sudbury is at the start of one of these, which has two loops (to Lavenham and Bures).

While there are numerous local cycle rides, a couple of the best in the area are:

1. The Heart of Suffolk Tour

A 31-mile (50km) circular route taking in some of the highlights of the south Suffolk countryside. The tour starts in the Market Square at Lavenham and progresses through Brent Eleigh, Milden, Groton, Boxford, Polstead, Hadleigh and Kersey, before returning along the B1115 to Lavenham.

2. The Painter's Trail

A 69-mile (111km) circular route through the Stour Valley and Dedham Vale taking in the bottom fringe of south Suffolk.

The local Tourist Information Centres can provide route maps for all of the cycle routes mentioned above.

Car Tours

With the exception of the A14 and A134, which both run from Colchester to Bury St Edmunds and encircle the area, most south Suffolk roads are comparatively slow and meandering. As such, they make leisurely car tours both enjoyable and worthwhile. One of the best tours is the scenic route from Sudbury to Needham Market. This covers some 22 miles (35km) and should take between two to three hours, allowing for sightseeing along the way.

Local roads should be followed to reach both Long Melford and Lavenham from Sudbury. From Lavenham, the A1141 takes in Brent Eleigh and Monks Eleigh, before joining the B1115 towards Chelsworth. The B1115 should be followed for a short distance prior to joining the B1078. The latter then passes through Nedging Tye, Great Bricett, Ringshall Stocks and Barking before arriving at Needham Market.

Public Transport

South Suffolk is reasonably well linked by road, rail, air and sea services. The A14 and A134 roads both connect to the main A12 route southwards to the M25. The A14 beyond Bury St Edmunds also provides a good route to the Midlands and the North.

The rail service from Ipswich to London is frequent and fast enough to attract commuters to live in the area. In addition, the whole of the line from Ipswich to Norwich is now electrified, which has further improved rail links. The line passes along the edge of south Suffolk and includes convenient stations at Needham Market and Stowmarket.

Sudbury also has a station. This is on the Gainsborough Line, which runs through to Marks Tey and connects with the main line service into London Liverpool Street.

Most of the south Suffolk area is reasonably accessible from either Norwich Airport or London Stansted. The proximity of the port of Harwich also makes sea crossings to Europe relatively easy (see Chapter 2).

As outlined in earlier chapters, there are good bus and community transport services across the county.

Places To Visit

(W) = Suggestions for wet days
(C) = Good entertainment value for children

Baylham House Rare Breeds Farm (C)

Mill Lane, Baylham, IP6 8LG
☎ (01473) 830264/563
www.baylham-house-farm.co.uk
Working livestock farm with breeding animals to feed, picnic areas and riverside walks.
Open: 11am–5pm Feb–Oct.

Gainsborough's House (W)

46 Gainsborough Street, Sudbury, CO10 2EU
☎ (01787) 372958
www.gainsborough.org
Gainsborough's House is the birthplace museum of Thomas Gainsborough, one of Britain's greatest painters.
Open: 10am–5pm Mon–Sat.

The Guildhall of Corpus Christi (W)

Market Place, Lavenham, CO10 9QZ
☎ (01787) 247646
Superb early-sixteenth-century timber-framed building with local museum, tearoom and giftshop.
Open: 11am–5pm Mar–Oct Tue–Sun & BH Mon. 11am–4pm Nov Sat & Sun.

Hadleigh Guildhall (W)

Market Place, Hadleigh, IP7 5AF
☎ (01473) 827752
www.hadleigh-guildhall.co.uk
Medieval timber-framed building dating from the fifteenth century.
Open: 2pm–5pm Thu & Sun Jul–Sep.

Little Hall, Lavenham (W)

Market Place, Lavenham, CO10 9QZ
☎ (01787) 247179
www.littlehall.org.uk
Fourteenth-century hall house restored in the 1930s and filled with a collection of art and artefacts.
Open: 2pm–5.30pm Easter–Oct Wed, Thu, Sat & Sun. 11am–5.30pm BHs.

Kentwell Hall (W) (C)

Long Melford, CO10 9BA
☎ (01787) 310207
www.kentwell.co.uk
One of England's finest sixteenth-century houses. Has one of the biggest living history events programmes in the UK.
Open: 12pm–5pm Apr–Sep. See website for other events.

Melford Hall (W) (C)

Long Melford, CO10 9AA
☎ (01787) 379228
www.nationaltrust.org.uk
Turreted brick Tudor mansion. Garden contains spectacular specimen trees.
Open: 1.30pm–5pm Apr Sat & Sun. May–Sep Wed–Sun. Oct Sat & Sun.

Needham Lake and Nature Reserve (C)

On the outskirts of Needham Market
☎ (01449) 724633
Local Nature Reserve with lake, walks, children's play area and picnic spots.
Open: Daily.

Museum of East Anglian Life (C)

Iliffe Way, Stowmarket, IP14 1DL
☎ (01449) 612229
www.eastanglianlife.org.uk
Discover the old East Anglia on this seventy-acre (28ha) site.
Open: 10am–5pm Apr–Oct Mon–Sat. 11am–5pm Sun.

The area covering Bury St Edmunds and west Suffolk has a fantastic variety of landscapes – from the chalk downlands of Newmarket, through the rich agricultural fenlands in the west, to the sandy brecklands of the north and its large lowland forest. Visitors can experience some of Suffolk's ancient past – with sites and relics from the Stone Age to the Iron Age – and discover much more of its recent history and heritage. From horse racing and aviation to country parks and stately homes, the area is both diverse and enthralling.

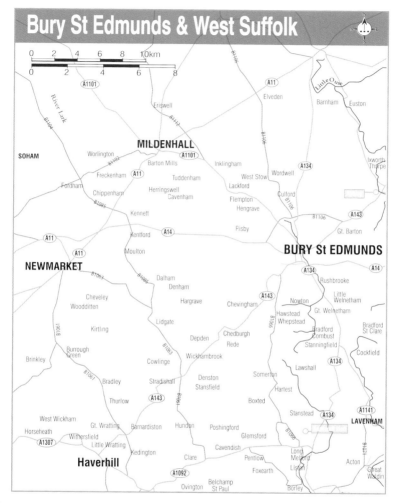

Bury St Edmunds & West Suffolk

(Map showing: A1101, Eriswell, Elveden, Barnham, Euston, Little Ouse, River Lark, MILDENHALL, A1101, Inklingham, West Stow, Wordwell, A134, Ixworth Thorpe, SOHAM, Worlington, Barton Mills, Freckenham, A11, Tuddenham, Lackford, Flempton, Culford, B1106, Chippenham, Herringswell, Cavenham, Fordham, Kennett, Hengrave, A143, Gt. Barton, Kentford, A14, Risby, BURY St EDMUNDS, A11, Moulton, A11, A134, A14, NEWMARKET, Dalham, Denham, Rushbrooke, Cheveley, Woodditten, Hargrave, Chevingham, A143, Nowton, Little Welnetham, Gt. Welnetham, Hawstead, Whepstead, Bradford Combust, Bradford St Clare, Kirtling, Lidgate, Depden, Chedburgh, Rede, Stanningfield, Cockfield, Brinkley, Burrough Green, Cowlinge, Wickhambrook, Lawshall, A134, Bradley, Stradishall, Denston, Stansfield, Somerton, Hartest, Thurlow, A143, Boxted, Stanstead, A134, A1141, LAVENHAM, West Wickham, Gt. Wratting, Barnardiston, Hundon, Poshingford, Glemsford, Horseheath, Withersfield, Little Wratting, A1307, Kedington, Cavendish, Long Melford, Acton, Great Waldin, Haverhill, Clare, Pentlow, Foxearth, Liston, A1092, Belcharmp St Paul, Ovington, Borley)

Bury St Edmunds

Bury St Edmunds has a long history, from its earliest roots as a Saxon settlement through to its modern-day position as a prosperous centre for brewing, manufacturing and tourism. The fortunes of the Abbey Church of St Edmund, in particular, have been closely intertwined with those of the town, and the expansion and prosperity of the settlement in the middle ages owed much to the control and patronage of the abbots who resided there.

It was in the eleventh century that King Canute replaced the existing monastery of Bury St Edmunds with an abbey. Two centuries before this, the remains of **King Edmund** had been brought to the site, giving the town its modern name. As an institution of considerable power and influence, the abbey grew enormously wealthy and alongside it Bury thrived as a medieval trading centre and a popular destination for pilgrims, keen to visit the remains of St Edmund.

By the twelfth century, the population of the town had reached 4,000 and wool manufacturing and related crafts had become the mainstay of the local economy. But Bury St Edmunds had also emerged as a major religious and political centre, and in 1214 played host to an important meeting of English barons, who swore an oath in the Abbey to compel the King to agree to the terms of Magna Carta. From that time the town has proudly broadcast its motto: 'Shrine of a king, Cradle of the law.'

A visit to the town today is not

St Edmund – Martyred King

The Vikings had a huge impact on the cultural diversity of the East Angles, but not without fierce hostility from the incumbent tribes. As an independent kingdom, East Anglia was ruled at that time by a young, unmarried king in his late twenties. And who better to rule and defend the vulnerable coastline than Edmund, a compassionate king whose Old English name meant 'noble protection', and whose reputation as a man of incomparable size and stature was legendary? The story of Edmund's resistance to the Vikings, his ultimate demise and later veneration as a Christian martyr is a story well established in Suffolk history.

King Edmund bravely led his followers in an ultimately unsuccessful campaign to oust the Vikings from East Anglia from the Autumn of AD869. His dishevelled army was eventually surrounded in the village of Hoxne, where the Norsemen offered Edmund a deal; to become a puppet-king under heathen rule or to die. Refusing steadfastly to renounce his Christian faith, Edmund chose death. On 20 November – now celebrated as St Edmund's day – the Vikings bound the King, whipped and beat him with clubs and tied him to an oak tree. They then fired countless arrows at him before beheading the brave leader.

Edmund's remains were eventually interred in a large church in the royal village of Beodericsworth (renamed Bury St Edmunds), becoming a site of pilgrimage for Christians from across Europe. In the tenth century, Edmund was declared the first Patron Saint of England. The story of his murder at Hoxne was given greater credence in the nineteenth century, when the oak tree, which believers claimed he had been tied to over a thousand years before, fell to the ground. When sawn up, it was found to contain a Danish arrowhead – evidence perhaps of the torture inflicted on the martyred king.

complete without a trip around **Ed-mundsbury Cathedral** and the stunning **Abbey Gardens.** The cathedral was built by Abbot Anselm in the twelfth century and for many centuries remained the last incomplete cathedral in Britain. However, work has recently finished, topping the cathedral with a 140-foot (40m) Gothic-style tower that crowns the roofline of this magnificent building.

The Abbey Gardens are no less impressive and regularly win prizes for their floral bedding displays. There is free admission to these public gardens, which include a host of ducks, a children's play area, aviaries, tennis courts, putting and bowling greens, a teashop and a riverside walk leading towards a Local Nature Reserve known as **No Man's Meadows**.

Also within the grounds are the original fourteenth-century **Abbey Gatehouse** and the **Norman Tower**, built between 1120 and 1148 – the most complete surviving buildings of the original abbey complex. The **Great Churchyard**, which sits behind it, dates from the same period, but may have been part of a much earlier eighth-century settlement. This has some fascinating carved tombstones.

St Mary's Church, which is housed within the front right corner of the Abbey Gardens, was built in the period from 1290 and was the burial place of **Mary Tudor**, Queen of France and sister to Henry VIII. It is the third largest parish church in the country and has the second largest aisle. Its hammer-beam 'angel' roof is particularly distinctive.

A walk around Bury's central streets reveals many more fascinating buildings. In fact, the street map of the town has changed little in 900 years. On **Angel Hill**, opposite the abbey complex, is the **Angel Hotel**, a former coaching inn from 1452 made famous by **Charles Dickens** in *The Pickwick Papers*. Nearby is the **Athenaeum**, in which Dickens once gave public readings.

A short walk further on from Angel Hill down Crown Street brings visitors to the **Theatre Royal**, the only surviving Regency playhouse in Britain. Very close to this is the **Greene King Visitor Centre**, which provides a fascinating insight into the local brewing industry that has flourished in the town for many centuries. Visitors interested in this should also seek out the **Malthouse Project** off Risbygate Street (on the opposite side of town), a former maltings building which houses a museum of original artefacts.

The **Buttermarket** and **Cornhill** area also holds many treasures. There is a twice-weekly market on the site and excellent shops, cafes, restaurants and public houses. One of the best hostelries here is the **Nutshell**, the smallest pub in Britain according to the Guinness Book of Records. More formal visitor attractions include the **Corn Exchange, Art Gallery** and **Moyse's Hall Museum**. The latter is within one of England's rare surviving Norman houses and contains captivating collections of local crime and social history.

Other attractions in the town include the **Suffolk Regiment Museum** on Newmarket Road and **Nowton Park**, which has 200 acres (80 hectares) of landscaped grounds. **Hardwick Heath**, off Hardwick Lane, also provides a perfect retreat from the bustle of the town, and has a tree gallery and some 200-year-old cedars.

Parking in Bury St Edmunds is abundant and inexpensive. For families there is a good **Leisure Centre** on Beetons Way, a local skate park and a number of children's recreation and play areas.

In addition to its fixed attractions, the town also has a full calendar of seasonal events throughout the year, including the **Bury St Edmunds Festival** – one of East Anglia's premier arts events each May.

Outside Bury St Edmunds

Bury St Edmunds is easy to reach by road and rail and provides an excellent base from which to explore the surrounding area of west Suffolk. Within a 10-mile (16km) radius of the town there are numerous visitor attractions.

Two miles (3km) east is **Rougham Airfield**, the home of the 94th Bomb Group of the United States Army Air Force in World War II. The wartime control tower still stands and is being restored as part of the **Rougham Control Tower Museum**. The airfield has a number of **open days and special events** featuring wartime aircraft, music, 1940s memorabilia and a range of activities for all the family.

To the north-west is the **Lackford Lakes National Nature Reserve**, a wetland habitat with several hides and an abundance of wildlife all year round. A visitor centre on the site provides stunning views across the reserve and an extensive programme of seasonal events.

Within 3 miles (5km) of this is the **West Stow Country Park and Anglo-Saxon Village**. This exceptional attraction features a reconstructed Anglo-Saxon village on the site of an original settlement. Finds excavated from the site can be seen in the Anglo-Saxon centre. The village is set within a 125-acre (50-hectare) country park containing a river, lake, heathland, woodland, nature trail and walks. It also has a cafe/shop and children's play area.

To the south-west of Bury is the attractive village of **Horringer**. Its village green is dominated by the fourteenth-century church of **St Leonard** (the patron saint of prisoners). The settlement has a long history and, in AD959, was owned by Theodred, the Bishop of London. In his will he bequeathed the land to the Abbey of Bury St Edmunds, who retained ownership for the next 600 years.

The village green is also the entrance to **Ickworth House**, one of the most extraordinary houses in England, with its rotunda and adjoining semicircular

The Nutshell Public House, Bury St Edmunds

Edmundsbury Cathedral, Bury St Edmunds

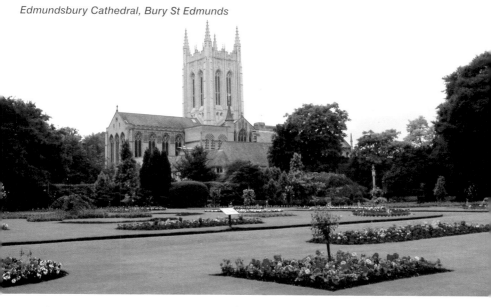

wings. Now owned by the National Trust, it still contains a large selection of paintings (including examples by Titian, Gainsborough and Velázquez) and Georgian silverware. The grounds, which were the work of **Capability Brown**, include an Italianate garden, vineyard, canal, lakeside walk and woodlands totalling over 100 acres (40 hectares).

Six miles (10km) south of Ickworth on the B1066 is the picturesque village of **Hartest**. There are stunning views from the hills surrounding the village, which could easily be mistaken for an area of the West Country. The settlement has existed for over a thousand years and there are several medieval buildings clustered around The Green which were once the shops and businesses of its thriving community. Also on The Green is the intriguing **Hartest Stone**, a mysterious limestone boulder that was discovered in a field at Somer-ton and dragged to its present position by a team of horses (see feature box on page 50).

The **Crown Inn** provides good food and ale and was original the **Moot Hall.** Like some other buildings in the village, it bears the mark of a private fire insurance company on its gable end from the days when the village had its own privately subscribed fire brigade. Close to the village is **Hartest Wood**, which is cared for by the Woodland Trust. This was planted up as native broadleaved woodland in 1999 and has an information board near its main entrance explaining the layout of the site.

Long Melford to Haverhill

The A1092 route that heads westwards from village of Long Melford is one of the prettiest stretches of road across any area of Suffolk. The picture postcard beauty of **Cavendish**, in particular, is one view that visitors should not miss.

The village was home to **Sir John Cavendish**, an ancestor of the Dukes of Devonshire. In 1381 local peasants, incited by **Wat Tyler**, burnt the mansion of Sir John, then Lord Chief Justice of England. He was later beheaded by a mob in Bury St Edmunds and avenged by his son, who eventually killed Tyler at Smithfield. Sir John's brother **Thomas Cavendish** also led a colourful and eventful life (see feature box below).

One of the best-known views of Cavendish looks across the village green and on to the **Pink Cottages**, behind which lies **St Mary's Church.**

The village has many other fine buildings and some excellent public houses. Nearby is **Nether Hall**, the home of **Cavendish Manor Vineyard**, which has a shop and information centre. Visitors can take part in wine tasting and walk around the fifteenth-century manor.

Further along the A1092 is the equally appealing village of Clare. This has a fine array of antique shops, art galleries, coffee houses and traditional pubs. The small market town, at the head of the River Stour, once held an important commercial position as the gateway to East Anglia. Its name is a reference to the 'clear' waters of the river.

The village has a number of historic buildings. Friars first came to the area in 1249 and the **Priory Buildings**

Thomas Cavendish – Pirate and Explorer

Thomas Cavendish (1555–92) was born in Trimley St Martin near Ipswich. He is famed for being the third circumnavigator of the globe after Ferdinand Magellan and fellow Englishman Sir Francis Drake. One of his early voyages was to America, where he sailed with Sir Richard Grenville and helped to start English settlements of Virginia in 1585.

Alongside his undoubted prowess as an explorer, Cavendish also revelled in the legalised piracy he was able to carry out as an Elizabethan privateer. The booty he captured helped to replace the fortune he had already inherited and squandered. In 1586 he sailed with three ships for the Pacific, where he burned three Spanish towns and thirteen ships before seizing the *Santa Anna* off Acapulco. This was loaded with gold and silk. When he returned to England in 1588, via the Cape of Good Hope, he was knighted by Queen Elizabeth I.

Finding himself short of money for a second time, the Elizabethan playboy planned a further circumnavigation in 1591. This ended in disaster when his fleet of five ships was dispersed in storms near the Straits of Magellan. Against the advice of Captain John Davys, Cavendish decided to take his ship and slip away from the others in the night and return home. He died at sea in the North Atlantic in May 1592. The remaining four ships arrived in Ireland in June 1593. Of the seventy-six sailors who had left England with Cavendish, only fifteen survived the journey.

include the remains of an earlier church and cloisters. **Nethergate House**, the parish church of **St Peter and St Paul,** the **Old Guildhall** and **Ancient House** all testify to the enormous wealth created by Clare as a wool town. The latter – also the **Town Museum** – contains a fine example of local pargeting work (see feature box on p64).

The **Old Maltings** (now a private home) and **Grove House** (originally Hall House and once used by a wheelwright) illustrate some of the earlier agricultural trades practised in the village. Nineteenth-century buildings include the former **Police Station**, old **Primary School and Railway Station** (now a visitor centre).

Clare Castle Country Park is Suffolk's oldest public country park. With twenty-five acres (10 hectares) of walks and woodland, it boasts the remains of a **Norman castle** with earthworks, motte and moats. The River Stour also flows through the park, together with nearly half a mile (700m) of mill stream.

Nearby **Stoke-by-Clare** is yet another pretty village. This has a lovely green and some good public houses. The fifteenth-century church of **St John the Baptist** contains a fascinating sixteenth-century **doom painting** that was uncovered in the 1940s.

The A1092 eventually joins the A1017 road into Haverhill.

Haverhill to Newmarket

Haverhill has been a market town for almost a thousand years. Its growth came largely as a result of the county's thriving textile industry, and by the nineteenth century the town had become a major centre for the production of drabbet smocks worn by agricultural workers.

One of Haverhill's key textile businesses was D Gurteen & Sons, a fustian manufacturer first established around 1784. The firm, which still exists today, expanded rapidly from 1856, creating a new mill plant with thirty-two steam-driven power looms. With this injection of capital, the Victorian town prospered and by 1900 its population had doubled to around four thousand and new homes, churches, schools and public buildings had been built to meet the needs of the growing community.

Fire destroyed most of Haverhill's older buildings in 1665. However, **Anne of Cleves' House** – which once formed part of the dower of the Queen Consort of England – has been completely renovated. This is on Hamlet Road and is now a physiotherapy clinic.

Most of the other historic buildings in the town are Victorian, including the imposing Gothic **Town Hall**, which was built by the Gurteen family. It is now a thriving **Arts Centre** and home to the **Haverhill Local History Centre**. This has an exhibition and study centre with materials relating to the heritage of the town and its surrounding area. Included are over 6,000 photographs and other local memorabilia.

Haverhill has a busy part-pedestrianised shopping area with major high-street retailers, a large number of shops and a regular market. Alongside its Arts Centre (which acts as a theatre and cinema), the town has a well-equipped **Leisure Centre** and **Ten Pin Bowling Alley**.

One of the more recent leisure developments is the **East Town Park**, a fifty-acre (20-hectare) site of meadows and trees. This is open all year round and boasts a children's play area, maze, easy access trail (suitable for wheelchairs, pushchairs and people with reduced mobility) and picnic area.

The town's seasonal events include an annual **Haverhill Festival**, which runs for two weeks in June and brings together a unique mix of music, film, comedy, dance, drama and community events. Many of these are free to attend.

Three miles (5km) north-east of Haverhill is the village of **Kedington**, which has links back to pre-Roman times and was mentioned in the Domesday Book. It sits on the River Stour and is home to the magnificent medieval church of **St Peter and St Paul**. Inside, the church contains a three-tier Jacobean pulpit and monuments to the local Barnardiston family.

Cowlinge, some 7 miles (11km) north of Kedington, is another tranquil and out-of-the-way Suffolk hamlet. It has a number of attractive thatched cottages, a medieval church and a good village pub. The annual **Open Gardens Day** is a very popular event towards the end of July and attracts a fair number of visitors.

North-west of Cowlinge, across an encroaching area of Cambridgeshire, is the world-renowned town of **Newmarket**. After Bury St Edmunds, this is the largest town in the west of Suffolk and, as the international home of horse racing, attracts visitors from all over the globe. Aside from its equine heritage, the town has some magnificent buildings, wonderful views and excellent shopping facilities.

King Charles II was a frequent visitor to Newmarket, drawn by his love of horse racing and making the town truly fashionable. The town's royal history is apparent at every turn. On Palace Street is the seventeenth-century **Palace House**, which was Charles' Newmarket home. This was restored in the 1990s and now houses many temporary exhibitions including paintings, crafts and clothing. The building is also home to the local **Tourist Information Centre**.

Newmarket has one long **High Street**, at one end of which lies its **Jubilee Clock Tower.** Further into town is the main shopping area of **Market Square**. The most imposing building on the High Street belongs to the Jockey Club and houses the **National Horseracing Museum**. This tells the story of horse racing over 400 years and includes art, memorabilia and trophies. The museum also organises a number of equine tours.

Racehorses are bred, stabled, traded, trained and raced in Newmarket and the industry dominates much of the workings of the town. Visitors can visit the home of the **National Stud** and race meetings are frequent on nearby **Newmarket Heath**. These are held on the **July Course** and the **Rowley Mile**. The first recorded race on the heath was in 1622. The two courses are separated by the **Devil's Dyke**. This large earthwork starts in neighbouring **Wood Ditton** and ends in **Reach**, a distance of over 8 miles (13km). It is a popular area for walkers.

Newmarket has its own **Leisure Centre** and a wide range of restaurants and public houses. Other attractions close to the town include the **Moulton Packhorse Bridge** – a medieval four-arched bridge over the River Kennett on the old route from Cambridge to Bury St Edmunds.

Newmarket to Brandon

Tuddenham Mill lies nine miles (15km) to the north-east of Newmarket. This late-eighteenth-century watermill was worked until the 1950s and was later converted into a restaurant. Today it is a fine hotel, retaining its exposed beams and iron waterwheel.

Mildenhall is just over 3 miles (5km) away. The parish is one of the largest

Forest at Brandon

in Suffolk and has Anglo-Saxon roots, although the area is better known for its ancient past. Some of the best discoveries in Europe of Stone Age tools have been made close to Mildenhall and there is also evidence of Bronze and Iron Age settlement. However, the town's biggest claim to fame is the discovery of the **Mildenhall Treasure** during the 1940s.

In 1931 Mildenhall was selected to

Ancient House, Clare

The Mildenhall Treasure

The Mildenhall Treasure is a major hoard of thirty-three Roman silver objects discovered in January 1942 by a Suffolk ploughman, Gordon Butcher, who removed it from the ground with help from Sydney Ford. They did not recognise the objects for what they were, and it was some years before the hoard came to the attention of the authorities. In 1946 the discovery was made public and the treasure was acquired by the British Museum in London. The treasure is believed to have been buried in the fourth century and is thought to have been of Mediterranean origin. It includes some of the finest surviving examples of Roman silversmithing, including a mid-fourth-century Great Dish.

be the home of one of the Royal Air Force's new-style bomber bases, which opened in 1934. In the same year the town hosted the **Mildenhall to Melbourne Air Race**, which attracted enormous international interest and brought in large crowds keen to see famous fliers like Amy Johnson. Today, the town retains its aviation links and RAF Mildenhall is now home to the United States Army Air Force.

The town's rich history is brought to light in the **Mildenhall and District Museum** on King Street. This has a replica of the Mildenhall Treasure and a wealth of local history.

Mildenhall's retail area is centred around its hexagonal **Market Cross**, where Friday markets have taken place since the fifteenth century and still continue today. The area also has some fine timber-framed buildings and an interesting **Town Pump**. The town sits on the banks of the River Lark and has a number of pleasant river walks. A stroll around the town will also reveal a number of good shops, public houses, restaurants and leisure facilities.

To the north of Mildenhall is the small village of **Eriswell.** This has a long and colourful history and was listed in the Domesday Book. During the 1700s, the village was owned by the New England Company, which created a number of new thatched and flint-built homes to provide an income for people emigrating to the United States. NEC plaques can still be seen on some of the buildings to this day.

In 1863, the village was sold to **Prince Duleep Singh**, the last Sikh Maharajah of the Punjab, who transformed the vast area around his stately home in nearby Elveden into a favoured hunting ground for the Victorian elite. He was a favourite of Queen Victoria and served as a local magistrate. His gravestone lies in the local churchyard.

One of the highlights of this part of west Suffolk is an area known as **The Brecks**. This is one of the great natural areas of Britain, covering 370 square miles (940 sq km) across both Suffolk and Norfolk. It is a landscape of tranquil forest, open heathland and agricultural land, which is home to many unique or distinctive birds, animals and plants. It is also steeped in Stone Age history and has the Neolithic Flint Mine of **Grimes Graves** within its landscape.

The Brecks area contains a wide range of Local Nature Reserves including **Lakenheath Poors Fen**, **Wangford Warren, Pashford Poors Fen** and **Hurst Fen**. One of the other main attractions locally is the **High Lodge Forest Centre**, which provides facilities for walking, cycling, orienteering, picnicking and relaxing. The site is great for families and contains a children's maze, play area and a '**Go Ape**' tree-top climbing and adventure experience.

The market town of **Brandon** lies at the gateway to The Brecks. Stone, Bronze and Iron Age relics have all been found in and around the town and evidence of an Anglo-Saxon settlement was also discovered around **Staunch Meadow** on the southern bank of the River Ouse near Brandon Lock.

The town developed from this settlement – the site being the lowest convenient natural crossing point on the Little Ouse River – and Brandon became a busy inland port for barges navigating to King's Lynn. It also became the chief British centre of the fur trade and the last home of the gun flint industry.

The town had a devastating fire in 1789, which came close to wiping out the Ferry Street area – now the main **High Street**. A walk around the town reveals a number of impressive flint buildings, indicative of the importance of this local resource since Neolithic times.

Planted in the 1920s, Brandon is now surrounded by the country's largest pine timberland. Although a commercial enterprise, the area provides good opportunities for both conservation and tourism. One of its key attractions is the **Brandon Country Park**, which is situated just off the B1106 and was once the site of a country house and managed parkland. Like its sister site, the High Lodge Forest Centre, this provides facilities for a wide range of activities

including walking, birdwatching and mountain biking.

Brandon has its own railway station and is well served by shops and leisure facilities.

Walks in the Area

All of the market towns in west Suffolk have their own town trails and local walks. Some, like the one in Bury St Edmunds, can be booked with the local Tourist Information Centre to include Blue Badge guides.

There are also numerous walks, both long and short, around the High Lodge Forest Centre and Brandon Country Park, enabling walkers to explore the diverse area of The Brecks.

Some of the best longer walks in the area include:

1. The Lark Valley Path

A 13-mile (21km) route from Mildenhall to Bury St Edmunds, which includes riverside, woodland, heathland and parkland sections.

2. The Bury St Edmunds to Clare Walk

An 18-mile (30km) route through rural west Suffolk.

Route maps for all walks can be obtained from Tourist Information Centres.

Cycle Rides

The west of Suffolk has as many inviting cycle routes to explore as other parts of the county. The Brecks area, in particular, attracts large numbers of keen cyclists and both the High Lodge Forest Centre and Brandon Country

Park are enormously popular for mountain biking.

Brandon is also on the National Cycle Network as part of the Thetford to Downham Market section of Regional Route 30.

While there are numerous local cycle rides, a couple of the best in the area are:

1. Riding the Suffolk and Essex Border

A 32-mile (51km) circular route which starts and finishes in the historic town of Clare.

2. In and around Bury St Edmunds

A 21-mile (51km) circular route which starts and finishes at Nowton Park on the southern edge of Bury St Edmunds and takes in Horringer, Ickworth Park, Angel Hill, the Abbey Gardens and Rougham Control Tower.

The local Tourist Information Centres can provide route maps for all of the cycle routes mentioned above.

Car Tours

The west Suffolk area is ideal for car tours given the close proximity and clustering of the many visitor attractions around the market towns of Bury St Edmunds, Newmarket, Mildenhall, Haverhill and Brandon. However, for its overall scenic beauty and historic appeal, the car tour from Haverhill to Long Melford on the A1017/A1092 is hard to beat. This takes in the timeless charms of both Clare and Cavendish, two of Suffolk's most photographed villages.

Clare Village

Long Melford

Public Transport

The west Suffolk area is reasonably well linked by air, sea, road and rail services.

Bury St Edmunds is some 50 miles (80km) away from London Stansted and 47 miles (75km) from Norwich Airport. Cambridge City Airport, which provides services to the north, east and City of London for business travellers lies just 27 miles (43km) away.

Passenger ferries run from northern Europe to Harwich, which is some 40 miles (65km) to the south-east of Bury St Edmunds. This is approximately one and a half hours' journey by car.

By road, Bury St Edmunds is situated on the A14 at Junction 43, which has good links to all major trunk roads in the East of England and good connections to the North, South and Midlands. All of the major market towns in west

Suffolk have bus stations and Bury is serviced by National Express coach connections from all over the country.

As outlined in earlier chapters, there are also community transport services across the county.

Bury St Edmunds, Newmarket and Brandon all have their own railway stations. Bury is connected to Cambridge, Ipswich and the Norwich to London line.

National Horseracing Museum, Newmarket

Places To Visit

(W) = Suggestions for wet days
(C) = Good entertainment value for children

Brandon, High Lodge Forest Centre (C)

Off the B1107 Thetford to Brandon road
☎ (01842) 815434
www.forestry.gov.uk/england
Forest park in England's largest lowland pine forest. Walks, cycle trails, high ropes course, orienteering and adventure playground.
Open: 9am–5pm daily.

Bury St Edmunds Cathedral and Abbey Gardens

Abbey House, Angel Hill, Bury St Edmunds, IP33 1LS
☎ (01284) 754933
www.stedscathedral.co.uk
Magnificent cathedral with a new Gothic-style lantern tower. Beautiful floral displays in the Abbey Gardens and twelfth-century abbey ruins.
Open: Daily.

Clare Castle Country Park

Clare town centre
☎ (01787) 277491
Suffolk's oldest public country park. Twenty-five acres (10ha) of walks and woodland and the remains of a Norman Castle.
Open: Daily.

Ickworth House, Park & Gardens (W)

Horringer, Bury St Edmunds, IP29 5QE
☎ (01284) 735270
www.nationaltrust.org.uk/ickworth
Extraordinary house with Regency and eighteenth-century pictures and furniture. Beautiful park and gardens to explore.
Open: House 1pm–5pm Mar–Nov closed Wed & Thu. Gardens 10am–5pm Mar–Sep closed Wed & Thu, Oct–Feb 11am–4pm. Park open daily.

National Horseracing Museum (W)

99 High Street, Newmarket, CB8 8JH
☎ (01638) 667333
www.nhrm.co.uk
An opportunity to discover the story of British horse racing and ride a racehorse simulator.
Open: 11am–4.30pm Easter–Oct.

West Stow Country Park and Anglo-Saxon Village (W) (C)

Between Bury and Mildenhall
☎ (01284) 728718
www.stedmundsbury.gov.uk/weststow.htm
A unique reconstruction of an Anglo-Saxon Village built on an original archaeological site.
Open: 10am–5pm daily.

Getting There

Airports

Cambridge City Airport
☎ (01223) 373765

London Stansted Airport
☎ (0870) 000 0303

Norwich Airport
☎ (01603) 411923

Ferry Services

Stena Line, Harwich
☎ (0870) 570 7070

DFDS Seaways
☎ (0871) 522 9955

Rail Services

National Express East Anglia
☎ (0845) 600 7245

Tourist Information Centres

Lowestoft & North-East Suffolk

Beccles, The Quay
☎ (01502) 713196

Southwold, High Street
☎ (01502) 724729

Lowestoft, East Point Pavilion
☎ (01502) 533600

Ipswich & the Suffolk Coast

Aldeburgh, High Street
☎ (01728) 453637

Ipswich, St Stephen's Lane
☎ (01473) 258070

Felixstowe, Undercliff Road West
☎ (01394) 276770

Woodbridge, Station Buildings
☎ (01394) 382240

Flatford, Flatford Lane
☎ (01206) 299460

Central Suffolk

Stowmarket, Museum of East Anglian Life
☎ (01449) 676800

South Suffolk

Hadleigh, Hadleigh Library
☎ (01473) 823778

Sudbury, Town Hall
☎ (01787) 881320

Lavenham, Lady Street
☎ (01787) 248207

Bury St Edmunds & West Suffolk

Brandon, Brandon Country Park
☎ (01842) 814955

Mildenhall, Mildenhall Museum
☎ (01638) 715484

Bury St Edmunds, Angel Hill
☎ (01284) 764667

Newmarket, Palace House
☎ (01638) 667200

Getting About

Car Hire

There are numerous car hire companies covering the county. Prices vary from company to company, and depend not only on the size/model of the car, but the hire location as well (hiring at an airport is likely to be more expensive). A booking is usually secured by leaving a credit card number. Conditions of car rental vary – generally drivers are expected to have held a full driving licence for at least a year (some companies ask for 2 years). The average minimum age is 23 (lowest 21 years); the average maximum age is 70 (occasionally up to 80 years). Some of the larger hire companies include:

Avis Car Rental UK
Ipswich
☎ (0870) 608 6342

Enterprise Rent-A-Car
Bury St Edmunds ☎ (01284) 748784
Ipswich ☎ (01473) 740900
Hertz, Ipswich
☎ (01473) 688900

Thrifty Van & Car Rental
Bury St Edmunds ☎ (01284) 754943
Ipswich ☎ (01473) 240822
Lowestoft ☎ (01502) 580333

Community Transport

General Enquiries
☎ (0845) 606 6067

Maps

The Ordnance Survey Travel Map Tour Series is ideal for visitors wishing to find their way around Suffolk. As well as clear, easy-to-read mapping, the two sheets feature extra tourist information like theatres, cinemas, sports venues and museums.

The Tour Map for Suffolk is produced at 1:100,000 scale (1 inch to 1½ miles or 1cm to 1km). It features all of Suffolk and parts of neighbouring counties. Also included are town navigation maps for Bury St Edmunds, Sudbury, Newmarket, Stowmarket, Woodbridge, Ipswich, Felixstowe, Aldeburgh, Southwold and Lowestoft.

The maps are designed to take the strain out of planning trips – whatever the method of travel. Main and minor roads are all shown, to help plan the quickest, shortest or the most scenic routes for journeys within each area. Significant park & ride facilities are included too. For those not travelling by car, the maps also highlight bus, coach and railway stations.

Public Transport Services

Traveline East Anglia

Provides impartial journey planning information about all public transport services – buses, coaches, trains and ferries – across Suffolk.

☎ (0871) 200 2233

Where to Stay

There is accommodation available to suit all needs and budgets throughout Suffolk: luxury hotels, secluded country hotels, lodges for travellers, hospitable pubs, bed & breakfast in private houses, farm accommodation, self-catering cottages, caravan parks, campsites and youth hostels. The list below provides a sample of the accommodation available in each area covered by the guide. More extensive lists can be obtained from relevant Tourist Information Centres:

Lowestoft & North-East Suffolk

Caravan Parks and Camp Sites

Bungay, Outney Meadow Caravan Park
☎ (01986) 892338

Kessingland Beach
☎ (0871) 664 9749

Kessingland, Heathland Beach Caravan Site
☎ (01502) 740337

Farmhouse Stays

Halesworth, Wissett Lodge
☎ (01986) 873173

Oulton, Laurel Farm
☎ (01502) 568724

Hotels

Beccles, Waveney House Hotel
☎ (01502) 712270

Southwold, Swan Hotel
☎ (01502) 722186

Oulton Broad, Ivy House Country Hotel
☎ (01502) 501353

Self-Catering Accommodation

Brampton, Old Orchard Cottages
☎ (01502) 575880

Ugglleshall, Manor Farm
☎ (01502) 578367

Halesworth, Rumburgh Farm
☎ (01986) 781351

Ipswich & the Suffolk Coast

Caravan Parks and Camp Sites

Dunwich, Cliff House Park
☎ (01728) 830724

Ipswich, Orwell Meadows Leisure Park
☎ (01473) 726666

Felixstowe Beach Holiday Park
☎ (0845) 815 9735

Leiston, Cakes & Ale Caravan Park
☎ (01728) 831655

Farmhouse Stays

Darsham, Priory Farm
☎ (01728) 668459

Shotley, Hill House Farm
☎ (01473) 787318

Hotels

Aldeburgh, Wentworth Hotel
☎ (01728) 452312

Orford, Crown and Castle Hotel
☎ (01394) 450205

Hintlesham Hall
☎ (01473) 652334

Westleton, Crown Inn
☎ (01728) 648777

Self-Catering Accommodation

Darsham, Fox Cottage
☎ (01986) 785473

Dunwich, Little Dingle Cottage
☎ (01473) 414806

Youth Hostels

Blaxhall Youth Hostel
☎ (01728) 688206

Central Suffolk

Caravan Parks and Camp Sites

Wortham, Honeypot Camp & Caravan Park
☎ (01379) 783312

Wickham Market, Orchard Camp Site
☎ (01728) 746170

Farmhouse Stays

Elmswell Hall
☎ (01359) 240215

Eye, Athelington Hall
☎ (01728) 628233

Hotels

Eye, Cornwallis Country Hotel
☎ (01379) 870326

Framlingham Crown Hotel
☎ (01728) 723521

Self-Catering Accommodation

Badingham, Workhouse Cottage
☎ (01728) 688343

Sibton Green, Cosy Suffolk Cottages
☎ (0771) 152 6252

South Suffolk

Caravan Parks and Camp Sites

Edwardstone, White Horse Camp Site
☎ (01787) 211211

Little Cornard, Willowmere Caravan Park
☎ (01787) 375559

Stonham Aspal, Stonham Barns Caravan Park
☎ (01449) 711901

Farmhouse Stays

Hintlesham, College Farm
☎ (01473) 652253

Nayland, Gladwins Farm
☎ (01206) 262261

Hotels

Lavenham, Swan Hotel
☎ (01787) 247477

Long Melford, Black Lion Hotel
☎ (01787) 312356

Self-Catering Accommodation
Assington, Partridge End Cottage
☎ (01634) 250251

Milden Hall
☎ (01787) 247235

Lavenham, Orchard Cottage
☎ (01787) 211115

Bury St Edmunds & West Suffolk

Caravan Parks and Camp Sites
Bury St Edmunds, Brighthouse Farm
☎ (01284) 830385

Mildenhall, Willows Campsite
☎ (01638) 715963

**Mildenhall, Round Plantation
Caravan Club Site**
☎ (01638) 713089

Farmhouse Stays
Bradfield Combust, Church Farm
☎ (01284) 386333

Rede Hall Farm
☎ (01284) 850695

Hotels
Bury St Edmunds, Angel Hotel
☎ (01284) 714000

Tuddenham Mill
☎ (01638) 713552

Bury St Edmunds, Clarice House Hotel
☎ (01284) 705550

Self-Catering Accommodation
Brandon, Grandma's Cottage
☎ (01842) 811236

**Bury St Edmunds, Badwell Ash
Holiday Lodges**
☎ (01359) 258444

What to See and Do

Lowestoft & North-East Suffolk

Amusement & Activity Centres
Beccles, Waveney Cue Club
☎ (01502) 712298

Kessingland, Africa Alive!
☎ (01502) 740291

Lowestoft, Mayhem Adventure Play
☎ (01502) 533600

Lowestoft, Pleasurewood Hills
☎ (01502) 586000

Nicholas Everitt Park
☎ (01502) 523575

Southwold Maize Maze
☎ (0780) 106 5845

Arts & Crafts

Beccles, Winter Flora
☎ (01502) 716810

Chediston Pottery
☎ (01986) 785242

Halesworth Gallery
☎ (01986) 873064

Halesworth, New Cut Arts
☎ (01986) 873285

Lowestoft Porcelain
☎ (01502) 572940

Boating & Piers

Beccles, Aston Boats Ltd
☎ (01502) 713960

Beccles Quay
☎ (01502) 713196

Bungay Boat Hire
☎ (01986) 892338

Lowestoft, Autumn Broad Dayboats
☎ (01502) 589556

Lowestoft, Hoseasons
☎ (0870) 902 3113

Lowestoft Lifeboat Station Shop
☎ (01502) 531507

Lowestoft Lighthouse
☎ (01255) 245011
(pre-arranged visits only)

Lowestoft, Mincarlo Trawler
☎ (01502) 565632

Lowestoft South Peer, Heritage Quay
☎ (01502) 533600

Oulton Broad, Waveney River Tours
☎ (01502) 574903

Southwold, Coastal Voyager Boat Trips
☎ (0788) 752 5082

Southwold Lighthouse Tours
☎ (01502) 722576

Southwold Pier
☎ (01502) 722105

Southwold/Walberswick Ferry
☎ (01502) 478615

Country Parks

Somerleyton Hall and Gardens
☎ (0871) 222 4244

Eating Out

Barnby, The Swan
☎ (01502) 476646

Blythburgh, White Hart
☎ (01502) 478217

Golf Courses

Beccles Golf Club
☎ (01502) 712244

Bungay & Waveney Valley Golf Club
☎ (01986) 892337

Carlton Colville, Rookery Park Golf Club
☎ (01502) 509190

Halesworth Golf Club
☎ (01986) 875567

Southwold Golf Club
☎ (01502) 723234

Leisure & Sports Centres

Beccles Sports Centre
☎ (01502) 712039

Beccles Swimming Pool
☎ (01502) 713297

Bungay Swimming Pool
☎ (01986) 895014

Halesworth Swimming Pool
☎ (01986) 872720

Lowestoft, Waveney Sports & Leisure Centre
☎ (01502) 569116

Oulton Broad, Broadland Holiday Village Leisure Centre
☎ (01502) 517452

Museums & Historic Sites

Beccles & District Museum
☎ (01502) 715722

Bungay, Bigod's Castle
☎ (01986) 896156

Bungay Museum
☎ (01986) 893155

Carlton Colville, East Anglian Transport Museum
☎ (01502) 518459

Flixton, Norfolk and Suffolk Aviation Museum
☎ (01986) 896644

Halesworth (Holton), Airfield Memorial Museum
☎ (01986) 873262

Halesworth & District Museum
☎ (01986) 875351

Lowestoft and East Suffolk Maritime Heritage Museum
☎ (01502) 561963

Lowestoft Museum
☎ (01502) 511457

Lowestoft, Royal Naval Patrol Service
Museum
☎ (01502) 586250

Lowestoft War Memorial Museum
☎ (01502) 587500

Southwold, Alfred Corry Museum
☎ (01502) 722103

Southwold, Amber Museum
☎ (01502) 723394

Southwold Museum
☎ (01502) 723374

Nature Reserves and Wildlife

Carlton Marshes Nature Reserve
☎ (01502) 564250

Lowestoft, Foxburrow Wood
☎ (01473) 890089

Water Sports

Beccles Yacht Station
☎ (01502) 712225

Learn Scuba
☎ (0845) 257 0131

Mutford Lock
☎ (01502) 531778

Oulton Broad Yacht Station
☎ (01502) 574946

Southwold Harbour
☎ (01502) 724712

Oulton Broad, Suffolk Water Sports
Association
☎ (01502) 587163

Windmills & Watermills

Herringfleet Smock Drainage Windmill
☎ (01473) 583352

Holton Windmill
☎ (01986) 872367

Ipswich & the Suffolk Coast

Amusement & Activity Centres

Felixstowe, Manning's Amusement Park
☎ (01394) 282370

Felixstowe Snooker & Pool Club
☎ (01394) 276012

Ipswich, Landseer Play Centre
☎ (01473) 433661

Ipswich, Suffolk Ski Centre
☎ (01473) 602347

Ipswich Town Football Club Stadium
Tours
☎ (0870) 111 0555

Martlesham, Beacon Rally Karts
☎ (0845) 644 1592

Martlesham, Kidz Kingdom
☎ (01473) 611333

Martlesham, Kingpin
☎ (01473) 611111

Rendlesham Forest Centre
☎ (01394) 450164

Sutton Hoo Maze Adventure Park
☎ (01728) 688984

Arts & Crafts

Aldringham Craft Market
☎ (01728) 830397

Butley Pottery
☎ (01394) 450785

Darsham, Glynn Hugo Studio Pottery
☎ (01728) 668274

Ipswich, All Fired Up Ceramics Cafe
☎ (01473) 286142

Knodishall, J K Pottery
☎ (01728) 832901

Ballooning

Virgin Balloon Flights
Launch sites at the Suffolk Showground and Jimmy's Farm, Pannington Hall, Wherstead.
☎ (0870) 444 2768

Boating & Piers

Aldeburgh Lifeboat Station
☎ (01728) 452552

Deben Ferry
☎ (01394) 282173

Felixstowe, Old Times Boat Services
☎ (01394) 270106

Felixstowe/Shotley Gate/Harwich Ferry
☎ (0791) 991 1440

Orford, Lady Florence River Cruise Restaurant
☎ (0783) 169 8298

Orford, Regardless Excursion Boat
☎ (01394) 450169

Orwell River Cruises, Orwell Lady Excursions
☎ (01473) 258070

Waldringfield Boat Yard
☎ (01473) 736260

Eating Out

Martlesham, Red Lion
☎ (01394) 382169

Westleton, Crown Inn
☎ (01728) 648777

Yoxford, Satis House
☎ (01728) 668418

Golf Courses

Aldeburgh Golf Club
☎ (01728) 452890

Darsham, High Lodge Golf Course
☎ (0845) 199 2065

Felixstowe Ferry Golf Club
☎ (01394) 283060

Ipswich, Brett Valley Golf Club
☎ (01473) 310718

Ipswich Golf Club
☎ (01473) 727474

Melton, St Audry's Golf Club
☎ (01394) 380200

Rushmere Golf Club
☎ (01473) 725648

Thorpeness Hotel Golf Club
☎ (01728) 452176

Ufford Hotel Golf & Spa
☎ (01394) 382836

Waldringfield Heath Golf Club
☎ (01473) 736768

Witnesham, Flynn Valley Golf Club
☎ (01473) 785267

Woodbridge Golf Club
☎ (01394) 382038

Woodbridge, Seckford Golf Club
☎ (01394) 388000

Leisure & Sports Centres

Deben Swimming Pool
☎ (01394) 384763

Felixstowe, Brackenbury Sports Centre
☎ (01394) 270278

Felixstowe Leisure Centre
☎ (01394) 670411

Ipswich, Chantry Sports Centre
☎ (01473) 602962

Ipswich, Crown Pools
☎ (01473) 433655

Ipswich Fore Street Pool
☎ (01473) 433668

Ipswich, Gainsborough Sports Centre
☎ (01473) 433644

Ipswich, Maidenhall Sports Centre
☎ (01473) 433622

Ipswich, Northgate Sports Centre
☎ (01473) 433611

Ipswich, Whitton Sports Centre
☎ (01473) 433633

Leiston Leisure Centre
☎ (01728) 830364

Museums & Historic Sites

Aldeburgh Museum
☎ (01728) 454666

Bawdsey Radar Station
☎ (0782) 116 2879 (to arrange special visits)

Dunwich, Greyfriars
☎ (01473) 583123

Dunwich Museum
☎ (01728) 648796

Felixstowe, Landguard Fort
☎ (0774) 969 5523

Felixstowe Museum
☎ (01394) 672284

Flatford, Bridge Cottage
☎ (01206) 298260

Ipswich, Clifford Road Air Raid Shelter Museum
☎ (01473) 251605

Ipswich, Christchurch Mansion
☎ (01473) 433554

Ipswich, Tolly Cobbold Brewery Museum
☎ (01473) 231723

Ipswich Transport Museum
☎ (01473) 715666

Leiston Airfield
☎ (01728) 602334

Leiston, Long Shop Museum
☎ (01728) 832189

Martlesham Heath Control Tower Museum
☎ (01473) 624510

Orford Castle
☎ (01379) 450472

Orford Museum
☎ (01394) 450295

Saxmundham Museum
☎ (01728) 663583

Snape Maltings
☎ (01728) 688303

Shotley, HMS Ganges Association Museum
☎ (01787) 228417

Woodbridge, Heavy Horse Museum
☎ (01394) 380643

Woodbridge Museum
☎ (01394) 380502

Woodbridge, Sutton Hoo
☎ (01394) 389700

Nature Reserves and Wildlife

Aldeburgh Haven Local Nature Reserve
☎ (01728) 453637

Aldringham-cum-Thorpe, RSPB North Warren
☎ (01728) 648281

Blaxhall Heath
☎ (01473) 890089

Bromeswell Green
☎ (01473) 890089

Dunwich, Dingle Marshes
☎ (01473) 890089

Felixstowe, Landguard Nature Reserve
☎ (01473) 890089

Melton, Foxburrow Farm
☎ (01473) 890089

Orford, Havergate Island
☎ (01728) 48281

Orford Ness National Nature Reserve
☎ (01394) 450057

Sizewell Belts, Nature Trail
☎ (01728) 831527

Westleton, RSPB Minsmere Nature Reserve
☎ (01728) 648281

Wherstead, Spring Wood
☎ (01473) 433995

Water Sports

Alton Water Sports Centre
☎ (01473) 328408

Woodbridge, Suffolk Water Sports Association
☎ (01394) 382007

Windmills & Watermills

Thorpeness Windmill
☎ (01394) 384948

Woodbridge Tide Mill
☎ (01728) 746959

Woodbridge, Buttrum's Mill
☎ (01473) 264755

Central Suffolk

Amusement & Activity Centres

Easton Farm Park
☎ (01728) 746457

Thornham Walks
☎ (01379) 788345

Stonham Barns
☎ (01449) 711755

Arts & Crafts

Badingham Bowling Green Crafts
☎ (01728) 638500

Debenham, Carters Teapot Pottery
☎ (01728) 860457

Farnham, George Cook, Basketmaker
☎ (01728) 603309

Swilland, Bernard Rooke Pottery
☎ (0776) 558 4643

Wattisfield, Henry Watson's Potteries
☎ (01359) 251239

Ballooning

Broadland Balloon Flights
Launch site at the Cornwallis Country Hotel, Brome, near Eye
☎ (01603) 495004

Boating & Piers

Sudbury, Rosette (River Tours)
☎ (01787) 313199

Country Parks

Haughley Park
☎ (01359) 240701

Helmingham Hall Gardens
☎ (01473) 890799

Eating Out

Eye, Queen's Head
☎ (01379) 870153

Laxfield, King's Head
☎ (01986) 798395

Golf Courses

Cretingham Golf Club
☎ (01728) 685275

Leisure & Sports Centres

Debenham Leisure Centre
☎ (01728) 861101

Stowmarket, Mid Suffolk Leisure Centre
☎ (01449) 674980

Framlingham Sports Centre
☎ (01728) 724374

Stradbroke Swimming Pool
☎ (01379) 384376

Museums & Historic Sites

Eye Castle
☎ (01449) 676800

Parham Airfield Museum
☎ (01728) 621373

Euston Hall
☎ (01842) 766366

Walpole Old Chapel
☎ (01986) 784412

Framlingham Castle
☎ (01728) 724189

**Wetheringsett, Mid-Suffolk Light
Railway Museum**
☎ (01449) 766899

Laxfield Museum
☎ (01986) 798318

Nature Reserves and Wildlife

Eye, The Pennings Local Nature Reserve
☎ (01449) 720711

Redgrave and Lopham Fen
☎ (01379) 688333

Monewden, Martin's Meadows
☎ (01473) 890089

Windmills & Watermills

Bardwell Windmill
☎ (01379) 251331

Pakenham Windmill
☎ (01379) 230277

Euston Watermill
☎ (01842) 766366

Saxtead Green Windmill
☎ (01728) 685789

Framsden Windmill
☎ (01473) 890328

Stanton Windmill
☎ (01359) 250622

Pakenham Watermill
☎ (01359) 270570

Thelnetham Windmill
☎ (01473) 727853

South Suffolk

Amusement & Activity Centres

Baylham House Rare Breeds Farm
☎ (01473) 830264

Arts & Crafts

Kersey Pottery
☎ (01473) 822092

Needham Market, Alder Carr Farm (Rural Crafts)
☎ (01449) 720820

Monks Eleigh, Corn Craft
☎ (01449) 740456

Ballooning

Virgin Balloon Flights
Launch sites at Elmsett Aerodrome and Stowmarket
☎ (0870) 444 2768

Boating & Piers

Flatford Boat Hire
☎ (01206) 298111

Flatford, Stour Trusty 11
☎ (01206) 392656

Eating Out

Kersey, Bell Inn
☎ (01473) 823229

Lavenham, Angel Hotel
☎ (01787) 247388

Lavenham, Great House
☎ (01787) 247431

Lavenham, Swan Hotel
☎ (01787) 247477

Golf Courses

Newton Green Golf Club
☎ (01787) 377217

Stoke-by-Nayland Golf Club
☎ (01206) 2628360

Stowmarket Golf Club
☎ (01449) 736473

Leisure & Sports Centres

East Bergholt Sports Centre
☎ (01206) 299340

Great Cornard Sports Centre
☎ (01787) 373132

Hadleigh High Leisure Centre
☎ (01473) 824441

Hadleigh Swimming Pool
☎ (01473) 823470

Holbrook Sports Centre
☎ (01787) 328317

Sudbury, Kingfisher Leisure Centre
☎ (01787) 375656

Museums & Historic Sites

Hadleigh Guildhall
☎ (01473) 827752

Lavenham, Guildhall of Corpus Christi
☎ (01787) 247646

Lavenham, Little Hall
☎ (01787) 247179

Long Melford, Kentwell Hall
☎ (01787) 310207

Long Melford, Melford Hall
☎ (01787) 379228

Stowmarket, Museum of East Anglian Life
☎ (01449) 612229

Sudbury, Gainsborough's House
☎ (01787) 372958

Wattisham Airfield Museum
☎ (01449) 678189

Woolpit & District Museum
☎ (01359) 240822

Nature Reserves and Wildlife

Bradfield Woods
☎ (01449) 737996

Cockfield, Bulls Wood
☎ (01473) 890089

Combs Wood
☎ (01473)890089

Hadleigh, Wolves Wood
☎ (01473) 328006

Needham Lake and Nature Reserve
☎ (01449) 724633

Windmills & Watermills

Drinkstone Mills
☎ (0784) 307 4700

Bury St Edmunds & West Suffolk

Amusement & Activity Centres

Brandon, High Lodge Forest Centre
☎ (01842) 815434

Bury St Edmunds, Activity World
☎ (01284) 763799

Bury St Edmunds, Green King Visitor Centre
☎ (01284) 714297

Bury St Edmunds, Ten Pin Bowling Centre
☎ (01284) 750704

Haverhill Snooker and Ten Pin Bowling Club
☎ (01440) 707774

High Lodge Forest Centre
☎ (01842) 815434

Arts & Crafts

Bury St Edmunds Art Gallery
☎ (01284) 762081

Horringer Crafts
☎ (01440) 712165

Long Melford, Posting House Pottery
☎ (01787) 311165

Long Melford, Withindale Gallery
☎ (01787) 311516

West Stow, Chimney Mill Galleries
☎ (01284) 728234

Country Parks

Brandon Country Park
☎ (01842) 810185

Clare Castle Country Park
☎ (01787) 277491

Ickworth House, Park & Gardens
☎ (01284) 735270

Knettishall Heath Country Park
☎ (01953) 688265

Eating Out

Bury St Edmunds, Angel Hotel
☎ (01284) 714000

Hartest, Crown Inn
☎ (01284) 830250

Golf Courses

Bury St Edmunds, Flempton Golf Club
☎ (01284) 728291

Bury St Edmunds Golf Club
☎ (01284) 755979

Clare Park Lake Golf Course
☎ (01787) 278693

Fornham St Genevieve, Suffolk Golf & Country Club
☎ (01284) 706777

Newmarket, Links Golf Club
☎ (01638) 663000

Newmarket, Royal Worlington & Newmarket Golf Club
☎ (01638) 712216

Leisure & Sports Centres

Brandon Leisure Centre
☎ (01842) 813748

Bury St Edmunds Leisure Centre
☎ (01284) 753496

Haverhill Leisure Centre
☎ (01440) 702548

Mildenhall Dome Leisure Centre
☎ (01638) 717737

Mildenhall Swimming Pool
☎ (01638) 712515

Newmarket Leisure Centre
☎ (01638) 662726

Newmarket Swimming Pool
☎ (01638) 661736

Museums & Historic Sites

Bury St Edmunds Cathedral and Abbey Gardens
☎ (01284) 754933

Bury St Edmunds, Moyse's Hall Museum
☎ (01284) 706183

Bury St Edmunds, Suffolk Regiment Museum
☎ (01284) 752394

Clare, Ancient House Museum
☎ (01787) 277662

Haverhill Local History Centre
☎ (01440) 714962

Ickworth House
☎ (01284) 735270

Mildenhall & District Museum
☎ (01638) 716970

Newmarket, National Horseracing Museum
☎ (01638) 667333

Rougham Tower Association
☎ (01359) 271471

West Stow Country Park and Anglo-Saxon Village
☎ (01284) 728718

Nature Reserves and Wildlife

Cavenham Heath
☎ (01284) 762218

Lackford Lakes Reserve
☎ (01284) 728706

Ixworth Thorpe Farm Nature Trail and Bird Reserve
☎ (01359) 269444

Lakenheath, RSPB Fen Nature Reserve
☎ (01842) 862036

Index

Index